T

with
wishes &
cheers &
beers)

Paul

Studies in European Fiction

Studies in European Fiction

❖

Swift-Voltaire, Fielding-Manzoni,
Dickens, a Dostoevsky Duo,
and Kafka

Paul Green

Permissions

For a number of reasons it was important to get the publication process of this book underway quickly, but requests for permissions to quote from the primary sources herein have been sent out as follows: (1) to Random House for the Modern Library editions of Swift's *Gulliver's, Travels, A Tale of a Tub, The Battle of the Books* and Dostoevsky's *The Brothers Karamazov* (C. Garnett translation); (2) to the Voltaire Foundation [at the Taylor Institution], University of Oxford, for *Les Oeuvres complètes de Voltaire;* (3) to Wesleyan University Press for Fielding's *A History of Tom Jones, A Foundling;* (4) to Garzanti Books S. P. A. for Manzoni's *I promessi sposi* (introduzione e note V. Spinazzola); (5) to Bantam Dell Publishing Group for Dickens's *Our Mutual Friend;* (6) to Penguin Books Ltd. for Dostoevsky's *Notes from Underground* and *The Double* (J. Coulson Translation); and (7) to S. Fischer Verlag GmbH for Kafka's *Sämtliche Erzählungen.*

Any stipulations made in relation to the rendering of permissions will be complied with by me as quickly as possible.

This book was printed in the United States of America.

To order additional copies of this book, contact:
Xlibris Corporation
1-888-795-4274
www.Xlibris.com
Orders@Xlibris.com
35539

CONTENTS

I

INTRODUCTION

The two comparative essays in this book were originally published in *Eighteenth-Century Salad with French and Italian Dressing: Swift-Voltaire, Fielding-Manzoni, and Reviews Franco-Italian and Italian* (Eugene, Ore.: Ye Olde XerOxenford Presse, 2003). The Dickens essay was published in *On Our Mutual Friend and Other Dickensiana* (same place, publisher, and year). The two Dostoevsky essays included herein were originally published in *From Russia with Love and a Literary Potpourri* (again same place, publisher, and date). The Kafka essay is an excerpted reworking from a longer essay in *Collected Writings on the Fiction of Franz Kafka, with a Germanics Supplement* (and again same place, publisher, date). With the exception of two republished articles by other hands at the end of the Dickens volume, everything in the four books cited above is my own work, and Ye Olde XerOxenford Presse is my limited-edition, xerox press.

The first essay in this book, the Swift-Voltaire one, was done later than the second, the Fielding-Manzoni. The problems involved in researching and writing the Swift-Voltaire essay, the immense task it was, are expounded in the final long endnote (note 87) to the essay, and given the extensiveness of that endnote, we can consider it the if-not-wholly provenance at least the history of the laborious process that went into the making of the essay, and to be properly introductory, I reproduce endnote 87 here:

> From its inception to its completion this essay has taken well over a
> year to do. I compiled over fifteen pages of bibliography on *Candide*,
> which was more than I needed, and a record thirty-three pages of
> bibliography on *Gulliver's Travels*, which was far too much. Needless
> to say, the process of researching all that bibliography required much
> time and labor, and when I got to the writing and documenting of

7

the essay, I had, to borrow a term from library science, extreme problems with bibliographic control. In some cases I searched until I found just what I needed. In some other cases the documentation is "for-example" documentation, and considerably more might have been added, And in some cases what I had absorbed in the process of doing research, as it were by osmosis, gets into the essay undocumented. And the writing of the essay was interrupted by the process of moving from Pullman, Washington, to Eugene, Oregon, and getting set up in Eugene. I have worked both long and arduously on this essay, and at that it is neither my longest essay nor does it have a record number of endnotes, but it has been as difficult an essay to write as any I have done.

When I began the task of collecting bibliography and, then in due course, material for the documentation of the Fielding-Manzoni essay I am not sure, but it most likely had begun as early as 1997, and for sure it had begun by the early months of 1998. I compiled fourteen pages of bibliography on *Tom Jones* and twenty-three pages on *I promessi sposi*, not as ungodly much as I compiled on Swift-Voltaire, but still a formidable amount, and furthermore the great majority of the Manzoni material was in Italian and not available at land-grant Washington State University's Holland Library, where I was doing my researching. And of course I could not even begin to try to obtain all the non-available material by means of interlibrary loan. On the other hand, so much of the Fielding material was available at Holland Library that I, by the time I had finished the xeroxing-some-articles and researching-the-rest process, the xeroxing having been done earlier and later the research having been done, and a rather lengthy process it was at that, in 1999 (and of course I also researched Fielding books), I had more material than I could use. Very early I discovered that one person before me at the least had thought of comparing *Tom Jones* and *I promessi sposi* and of speculating as to whether or not Manzoni had read *Tom Jones*. That person was one Antonia Mazza, and right away through ILL I got her article, "Coincidenze," which sees a couple of things I hadn't and otherwise is mostly sketchy. Then over an extended period of time I obtained thirty-four other articles through ILL, some in obscure journals but found somehow. One of circa forty-five pages and another of circa seventy-five pages, both very important in view of what I was to do in the essay, were kindly made available for me by the ILL staff at the University of Oregon's Knight Library's having sent the volumes in which the articles were on a short-term basis, and I am most grateful to the U of O ILL staff for those helpful services. The articles chosen were ones which seemed, by their titles, most needed or useful for my purposes. And as this ILL collection process was ongoing, I xeroxed all the articles on Manzoni available in Holland Library, mostly from the journal *Italica*, and I researched the relatively few Manzoni books available in Holland Library. I am very adept in researching at scanning through articles and in cases even books and plucking out notes and quotes, but such bulk of xeroxed material as I eventually collected (including that on *Tom Jones*) obliged a slow, even tedious, process of noting author (or adding a short title when the author published more than one thing pertinent) plus page number and note or quoted statement as I worked my way along. Then the process of documentation, for which purpose I had kept the articles in order, obliged locating articles to obtain article title, journal title, volume, year, and adding the page or pages cited in my notes as well as searching through two thick pads of Fielding notes or the note cards I had on Manzoni. Finally in the early months of 2001 the essay was finished, typed, and xeroxed copies of the typescript were made, and work on the essay, of course a several-years process, had been interrupted by the necessities of writing other things, some of which were published. Without these interruptions to take care of other, less arduous writing projects, this Fielding-Manzoni project would have been as taxing and exhausting as the almost uninterrupted, except for the period somewhat before and somewhat after my move from Washington State, years later, back to Oregon, Swift-Voltaire project. In either case the research for these long, comparative (and somewhat contrasting) essays was as extensive-intensive as that done for some books.

Most readers of these comparative-with-contrasts essays liked them but in a number of cases did not know some of the novels or novelistic works treated. *Recovering Literature* editor Gerald (Joe) Butler criticized Fielding-Manzoni rather severely, and I in reply criticized him rather severely. Butler is a Fielding authority, but his only direct criticism on my treatment of Fielding, as distinguished from his negative criticisms on the essay per se, was that I was reductive on the Richardson-Fielding animosity. Earlier that essay had been rejected by a *Comparative Literature Studies* reader fluent in Italian and inferably a fanatical Catholic. When I submitted the Swift-Voltaire essay to Butler for *RecL*, he said, reworked, possibly it could be published but complained that some of my comparisons were "termpaperish." And he is one of a number of readers who seemed to fail to see that in both essays I went to heroic lengths to come up with circa seventeen ways to compare the novels or novelistic works in question. The most I can assert with regard to Fielding-Manzoni is that there are affinities, some quite striking, whereas there are documentable influences of Swift on Voltaire. The editorializing-allusions-asides in these essays are from my experience as a man who has lived through much, literarywise and otherwise, *experience* is a prime category in the contextualist aesthetic-world view to which I adhere, and note that contextualism asserts spreading by strands and references, that resonances are compatible in it, and that it is not an aesthetic of narrow containment. When I in turn submitted Swift-Voltaire to *CLS*, I criticized the Fielding-Manzoni reader so savagely that the essay was returned with the comment that *CLS* had no reader suitable to go over the essay. Thus until now these two essays, into which so much labor, documentational and otherwise, and on which so much time was spent, have appeared only as limited-edition, xerox-press publications.

Last, in relation to these essays I must render two notes of thanks for help rendered. There are at times instances in which ILL requests, after having been duly searched, cannot be filled. I wish to thank David (Dave) Smestad, supersleuth ILL searcher at WSU Libraries, who most of all on Manzoni but also on other writers or writings, filled all of my requests. In fact, even for a Frank Norris article I did, when he couldn't obtain a copy of an English-language article in a Japanese journal which I needed, he wrote to a Japanese university requesting a copy. That university sent the request to another Japanese university, which supplied the copy for me. And so, Dave, my hat is off to you, and I give you many thanks. It has been almost exactly three years since I lost contact with my last remaining friend from UC Berkeley days, San Franciscan Thomas L. (Tom) Hargrove, who is or was inter alia a retired librarian. When I checked during a late 2004 Bay Area visit, I determined only that he was no longer living in his Russian Hill apartment. Near eighty years of age, with advanced diabetes, he may now be dead or at best clinging to life in a nursing home. I am still saddened by the loss of such a sterling friend, but I am glad I got a message of thanks to him before contact was severed. For over the years I am fairly sure that, at one time or another, I have read everything of Freud's except his letters. This I said in Swift-Voltaire and therein also said that I couldn't recall Freud's having mentioned Swift but that, at any rate, Swift was a precursor of Freud. Tom to the rescue, for he informed me that in *The Interpretation of Dreams* Freud in fact mentions Swift. Thus Tom was of crucial help here, and I, in my unknowing as to his fate, can only say, Tom, I bid you a mournful ave atque vale.

A wealth of material has accumulated on Dicken's *Our Mutual Friend*, and among all this there are of course variations in quality, pertinence, and scope. I try to be low key; one attempt to make this point, which may have been ineptly stated and which then concerned only my work, was taken by one person to be outrageously arrogant or excessive. I restate my point here, cautionarily drawing on the works of other writers, both published in *Nineteenth Century Fiction* (Stanley Friedman's "The Motif of Reading in *Our Mutual Friend*" [28 (1973), 38-61] and Rosemary Mundhenk's "The Education of the Reader in *Our Mutual Friend*" [34 (1979), 41-58]) and articles highly complementary albeit one is directed to the novel per se and the other towards enlightened reader responses to the novel. Thus these two if taken in tandem with—from my xerox-press Dickens book—my reproduced dissertation chapter on the violence in *OMF*, my republished "Two Venal Girls . . . ," article (studying a Zola girl as well as Bella Wilfer with a mounds-plot backdrop), and "Claustration and Openness . . . ," my essay reproduced in this book (studying Bradley Headstone and other river-plot characters), one can conceivably get a sweepingly comprehensive view of a novel noted for anal moneygrubbing and predation. A few quibbles have been raised about this latter essay, but I infer either *Studies in English Literature 1500-1900* or *English Studies in Canada* might have published it had there not been copyright complications. At any rate, this river-plot essay, being relatively short and highly focused, would generally pass muster for publishability as the two preceding comparative essays might not in the eyes of some.

Now we proceed to Dostoevsky and first to the *Notes* essay. One annihilating reader deemed this essay of no worth though several others seem to have found it worth their time to read. At any rate, it is an essay that I am glad I did, particularly in the first half I think that there is a great deal which is meaty, and when I reread this partially-forgotten essay before I included it in one of my xerox-press books, I saw that there is a fair amount of commentary in the second half of the essay and that the latter half is not a solid mass of quotations. The defense of intellectuality in the first half of the essay should have had with it a cautionary statement to the effect that most intellectuals just pimp to the system that obtains, but it was written in the spirit of Novalis's statement made more widely known by Walter Pater: "Philosophieren ist deflegmatisieren, vivificieren." Thus, I meant it in the sense by which intellectuality can enable one to rise above a business-as-usual doggy surface reality and to show it for what it in fact is. This might be considered a sort of metaphysic designed not to rise above the physical world per se but for the vantage to better see how much supposed to pass for reality is in fact fraud, etc. The *Karamazov* essay is manifestly dated, but in what it does it gives a very clear and trenchant direction for any supposititious or extensive or amplifying continuation. Especially I want to have the character studies at the end (or in the "Coda") be "of record." Whether I could have done as well on her as the critics quoted or cited did on Katya is a moot question. To readers of this becoming a bit impatient about the inclusion herein of given works which might be deemed in need of revision or updating, please pass over or through the next topic, Kafka, and you will see my reasons for doing as I am doing.

The "Strafkolonie" essay derives from a Kafka chapter in my dissertation, updated and somewhat revised it serves as the last section in "Three Kafka

Stories of Violence" in my above-mentioned Kafka-Germanics book, and among my various Kafka pieces it has generally been singled out as admirable though it has been pointed out to me—rather to my consternation—that Kafka tended to identify with the officer in the story whom I so take to task. The study of this story was excerpted, with appropriate changes made enabling it to stand alone, to follow out the possibility that a friend of a friend might get it published in Germany. That hope came to nothing, and my one attempt to get it published in a Germanics journal signaled, as in the case of the Dickens essay herein, that copyright complications would be an obstacle. It, again like the Dickens, is not overly long, very focused, and not highly conducive to the eliciting of complaints from readers. "Kafka" covers a fair range of things, but, to generalize, if one wants a ready means to blow his or her mind, then the thing to do is to steep him- or herself in Kafka.

At his death Dickens left incomplete a novel of which he had written circa 240 pages, *The Mystery of Edwin Drood*. A number of ambitiously audacious people have written and published endings for *Drood*. Of course no one can know precisely where Dickens would have taken Drood had he lived to finish it. But enough got written that scholars can make some inferences, especially that Drood, who disappears, has been murdered by cathedral organist John (Jack) Jasper, who, if my memory is correct, is an opium addict. Furthermore, it can be inferred that Dickens identified rather closely with Jasper because, first, having in his later works generally gone after his society with all guns firing, he felt himself a sort of criminal. And it is widely known that in his later public readings Dickens obsessively read the passage about the murder of Nancy from *Oliver Twist,* which is evidence of a high degree of sadism in him, and Michael Slater's inference in his *Dickens and Women* that Dickens likely never consummated his relationship with Ellen Ternan, justifiable causes for rage, and his driving himself to achieve make it very understandable that in the last stage of his life Dickens may have been visited often by murderous impulses. I tend to share this malign streak with Dickens for much the same reasons, Dostoevsky was markedly influenced by Dickens, and for better or worse I have to a certain extent a composite Dostoevskian character.

The just preceding likely seems informative, but readers may well wonder why I have taken this detour to Dickens, *Drood*, and beyond. So let us recapitulate quickly on the material in this book and make the connection or analogy. The Swift-Voltaire essay was finished about three-and-a-half years ago and the Fielding-Manzoni about four-and-a-half years ago. More has been written on these writers since, perhaps the likeliest complaint about both essays would be that they should be cut down, the Manzoni research was predominantly drawn from articles, etc., but these two essays as such are not terribly old or dated, they are more than extensively documented, and readers have seen to what lengths I had to go to document and write these essays. The situation with the two Dostoevsky essays is different because both essays were written over a decade ago but at least are documented amply enough to sustainedly marshal evidence or build satisfactory cases. The *Notes* essay especially might elicit some negative comments, I am further on now and might change a few things if I were to redo these essays, but in the main I stand by what I have said in these four essays as well as in the Dickens and Kafka and want them to be "of record" more extensively than in their prior most-modest publication. And now for the Dickens analogy. The opportunity to put together this book came very recently, it is important to get the publication process underway as quickly as possible, for my health has declined markedly in the past year and a half, I have advanced pulmonary disease as well as several other worrisome conditions, I can no longer count on a likely "world enough and time . . . ," I have other writing projects either on hold or in the works, including completion of research-rereading for a book on nineteenth-century poetry. A fair percentage of this writing may never have the opportunity to reach fruition. Thus the essays in this book are presented as such, they are the product of a formidable amount of work, they are here presented as such for readers, if they so choose, to do bibliographic updating, to do what readers and critics love to do, find things to carp or cavil or complain about in these essays, or to write critical essays and articles as responses. Hopefully I'll live long enough that this book's fate won't be Droodian. And as to whatever responses it elicits, if readers bother to respond, "Que sera, sera . . . ."

Earlier in this introduction I rendered three notes of thanks for help specific to the contents of this book. Also I render thanks for, through differences, developmental changes, at-present rare or intermittent contact, cessation of contact, etc., the general critical acumen I acquired by friendship with members of my old University of Washington circle. Most of all I should thank Joe Butler and Art Efron for steadfast and signal help and support over the years. Also I should render thanks to UW emeritus Wayne Burns, Jerry Zaslove, Donn and Carol Rawlings, Dan and Sharon Callahan, Mike Steig, Jim Flynn, and others of them with whom my only contact has been through their writings. Among other supportive and encouraging friends I must especially thank Barb Nakata and Richard Heinzkill. The great majority of my mentors who gave me illumination in various ways are now in their graves, and among them I should especially mention two whom I knew only through the medium of print: Stephen C. Pepper, who refined a contextualist dynamic out of a Deweyan matrix, and Norman O. Brown, who in his *Life Against Death* gave me my first real plunge into psychoanalysis and various and sundry other matters.

Eugene, Oregon 2006

II

GULLIVER'S TRAVELS AND *CANDIDE*:

AN INTERREADING

*G*ulliver's Travels* was published in 1726, and *Candide* was published in 1759. Voltaire had read and liked *Gulliver's Travels*, and although in any number of ways *Gulliver's Travels*, and *Candide* are very different works, Swift's work in ways influenced Voltaire in the writing of *Candide*. A. Owen Aldridge says:

> Unlike *Zadig* and Voltaire's other philosophical tales that
> have a protagonist but no other characters, *Candide* has a roster
> of personae. In this sense it is closer to a conventional novel than
> is *Gulliver's Travels*, the literary work which it resembles most and
> which served as a partial model.[1]

The question of the novel or the novelistic I shall defer till later. But Aldridge is not correct to say that *Zadig* has no other characters than its protagonist, and also *Micromégas* has a number of characters. Other critics than Aldridge have of course noted the influence of Swift and *Gulliver's Travels* upon Voltaire and *Candide*, but we can take Aldridge's statement as representative, and I think we may say that it is not most fruitful to try to find point-by-point influences but that it is better to find ways in which the two works are akin and to see ways in which the two works *resonate* to each other. Hence, I proceed.

[1.] *Voltaire and the Century of Light* (Princeton, NJ: Princeton UP, 1975) 252-53.

Gulliver's Travels and *Candide* are the two greatest satires of the eighteenth century. Voltaire's strengths are not in characterization, and most likely *Gulliver's Travels* is a greater work than *Candide,* but neither of these statements should in any way diminish the greatness of *Candide.* Aldridge says: "*Candide . . .* ranks as one of the masterpieces of European literature, not primarily because of style but because of its realistic portrayal of the human condition."[2] Realism we shall get to shortly, but what does *Candide* satirize? We find what it satirizes in this gem of a statement made by the philosopher G. W. Leibniz:

> To him [one M. Arnauld] I even tendered a Latin Dialogue of my own composition upon this subject, about the year 1673, wherein already I laid it down that God, having chosen the most perfect of all possible worlds, had been prompted by his wisdom to permit the evil which was bound up with it, but which still did not prevent this world from being, all things considered, the best that could be chosen.[3]

Now isn't that sweet? And how do people in our time who share Leibniz's views explain, for example, the existence of thousands of homeless people in American cities? In *Candide* the teacher of Candide, the fatuous Leibnizian Dr. Pangloss, even after all he goes through in the course of *Candide,* still proclaims, to quote his words early in the work, that this is "le meilleur des mondes . . . ."[4] I infer that Voltaire is not widely read anymore except of course by scholars and Voltaire specialists, but Theodore Besterman speaks of "*Candide,* the only one of Voltaire's innumerable writings which is still a best-seller . . . ."[5] Among all its readers, there are surely some who miss the fact that the work is "the profoundly pessimistic *Candide . . . ,*"[6] including scholars. And what is satirized in *Gulliver's Travels*? *Gulliver's Travels* has to be the greatest assault on human pretensions and pride or narcissism in all the annals of literature. That assault is not only

2. P. 260.
3. *Theodicy: Essays on the Goodness of God, the Freedom of Man, and the Origin of Evil* (La Salle, Ill.: Open Court, 1985) 67.
4. Citations from Voltaire in my text are to *Candide* in *Les Oeuvres complètes de Voltaire* (Oxford: The Voltaire Foundation at the Taylor Institution, 1980). Here p. 131. Further page references will be given in the text.
5. *Voltaire* (New York: Harcourt, Brace and World, 1969) 412. Besterman says relatively little on *Candide* in this hefty tome, but as far as I know, he is still the leading Voltaire scholar.
6. Besterman, p. 418.

present in the last book, Book Four, wherein the reader is unable to avoid noticing that his or her resemblance to the shitty Yahoos[7] is too close for comfort, but it is persistent also in the earlier parts, indeed throughout *Gulliver's Travels*. Gulliver returns from his last voyage both deranged and misanthropic. Was Swift also misanthropic? Frank Brady says: "He [Swift] calls his view of man a 'great foundation of misanthropy,' though of course he and his contemporaries considered misanthropy one of the worst vices."[8] Nonetheless, I think we can infer that a great deal of the time Swift must have been appalled at his fellow men. We have seen that *Candide* is still a popular work, and though *Gulliver's Travels* requires a perceptive adult reader for maximum comprehension, M. Sarah Smedman records that "*Gulliver's Travels*, like *Pilgrim's Progress* and *Robinson Crusoe*, has for more than two and a half centuries been a book read for pleasure by children."[9] Again, *Gulliver's Travels* is as great an assault on narcissism as one could ask for, and of course narcissism is not genital, and it is oral only when a person is talking narcissistically, so narcissism can be nothing other than anal.

Both *Gulliver's Travels* and *Candide* are travel books, and in *Gulliver's Travels* that fact is given in the title. But *Gulliver's Travels* is also a fantasy, and that topic I shall get to later, and so what is gained by its being a fantasy travel book? Of course we have seen that *Gulliver's Travels* is a mammoth assault on narcissism, so the course of Gulliver's travels is accordingly exceedingly instructive. Albeit Gulliver visits imaginary lands except for a brief stop in Japan in Book Three, in preparing himself to write the work Swift steeped himself in various accounts of travels, and in the journal *Notes and Queries* especially there are any number of notes about books which Swift read or most likely read, which would seem to have had some influence on *Gulliver's Travels*. Swift wrote Book Three of *Gulliver's Travels* after he had written Books One, Two, and Four, and by and large its status has been problematic, if not questionable, and John M. Munro speaks of the sophistication of

---

[7.] See passim Norman O. Brown's splendid chapter on Swift, "The Excremental Vision," in his *Life Against Death: The Psychoanalytical Meaning of History*, 2nd ed., introd. Christopher Lasch (Middletown, Conn.: Wesleyan UP, 1959) 179-201.

[8.] In his "Introduction" to *Twentieth-Century Interpretations of* Gulliver's Travels, ed. Brady (Englewood Cliffs, NJ: Prentice-Hall, 1968) 3.

[9.] "Like Me, Like Me Not: *Gulliver's Travels* as a Children's Book," in *The Genres of* Gulliver's Travels, ed. Frederik N. Smith (London and Toronto: Associated U Presses, 1990) 75.

the theories advanced by Kathleen Williams and John H. Sutherland, who both argue that Book III is an essential step in Swift's thematic scheme. Miss Williams notes that the book begins as a "voyage to illusion" and ends with Gulliver experiencing "a darker reality" than any he has yet encountered.[10]

Gulliver's visit to Glubbdubdrib in Book Three is hardly his most fruitful experience, but critics who defend Book Three usually point out that the book satirizes intellectual pride or narcissism, but if this book plunges Gulliver into "'a darker reality'" than any heretofore, it should be added that his experiences in Book Four cause him to return home deranged. At any rate and to recapitulate, Gulliver's visits to imaginary places are exceedingly instructive for Swift's readers. In "The Voyage in *Candide*" Ruth Plant Weinreb points out that

> If one traces a map of Candide's voyage, the thirty chapters fall roughly into three parts: the first third taking place in Europe, the second in South America, and the last once again in Europe.[11]

The first third of *Candide* is the part of the work in which by and large Candide undergoes his worst experiences. The last third, except for Candide's marriage to his once-beautiful Cunégonde who is now ugly and "acariâtre et insupportable" (p. 254), seems the least effective part of the work, but there is more to say. I quote two statements made by Nicholas Cronk. This is the first:

> Dr. [R. J.] Howells characterizes [Mikhail] Bakhtin's "spirit of carnival" as "a universal vision of festivity and excess, breakdown and renewal," but this is surely to underplay the crucial importance which Bakhtin attributes to the subversive function of the carnivalesque.[12]

And this is the second:

---

10. "Book III of *Gulliver's Travels* Once Again," *English Studies* 49 (1969): 430.
11. In *Approaches to Teaching Voltaire's* Candide, ed. Renée Waldinger (New York: Modern Language Association of America, 1987) 64.
12. "Voltaire, Bakhtin and the Language of Carnival," *French Studies Bulletin*, 18 (1986): 4.

> The carnival themes of *Candide* acquire intriguing ambivalence
> when placed in the context of Voltaire's dogmatic dismissal of a
> carnival of language.[13]

If Voltaire does not exactly use the language of carnival, there is nonetheless something of the spirit of carnival in Candide and Martin's travels in Europe in the last third of *Candide*.

We have seen that Aldridge notes the realistic portrayal of the human condition in *Candide*. And in the sense that *Candide* undercuts and deflates the fatuous optimism of a good many people and that *Gulliver's Travels* undercuts and deflates the too-common phenomenon of human narcissism, both are realistic works. But in another sense how can we consider *Gulliver's Travels* a realistic work when nearly everything in it is fantasy? Swift, or rather his narrator Gulliver, takes some special pains on that score. We can see these pains or efforts right from the start as in his letter to his cousin Richard Sympson Gulliver has purportedly been accused by Sympson of debasing human nature, and in his publisher's letter to the reader Sympson states that he knows Gulliver. Thus the fictional character Gulliver, in having a cousin who complains about Gulliver's purported literary opus and states that he knows Gulliver, attains a degree of "reality" or "authenticity" which redounds also to the "veracity" of his purported tale. But that is not all. Robert C. Elliott observes that "Gulliver . . . succeeds in the novelist's great task of creating the illusion of reality."[14] And how, Cousin Sympson aside and in the tale proper, does Gulliver, or Swift, do it? For one thing, Ronald Knowles says:

> *Gulliver's Travels* takes great pains to copy most seventeenth-century predecessors to establish a concrete geographical setting against which Swift can place fantastic materials for the ulterior purpose of satire.[15]

At least once in *Gulliver's Travels* Swift makes a geographical gaffe, but geography is a secondary concern, and though the reader knows all along that, as C[laude] J. Rawson says, "We are hardly expected to take *Gulliver's Travels* as a straight (even if possibly mendacious) travel story,"[16] Gulliver

---

13. P. 7.
14. In "The Satirist Satirized" in Brady, p. 48.
15. Gulliver's Travels: *The Politics of Satire* (New York: Twayne, 1996) 13.
16. *Gulliver and the Gentle Reader: Studies in Swift and Our Time* London: Routledge and Kegan Paul, 1973) 9.

takes even greater pains than geographical ones to try to convince the reader of his story's "actuality." It is in the *literalness* of Gulliver's account and in this related phenomenon discussed by Stephen M. Cohan that we get the work's "realism":

> Those many details which fill Gulliver's narratives . . . are used to create the illusion of reality by insisting that the *Travels* is not a fictional account at all . . . .
>
> This bombardment of detail, along with the many satiric elements, suggests the various tangible points of comparison between Swift's actual world and the ones of his making.[17]

When we sometimes see even the grimmest "naturalistic" novel called "illusionist," we can discern that in ways *Gulliver's Travels*, albeit "illusionistic," is in a sense "realistic." As I have said, Voltaire's strengths are not in characterization. And as the characters in *Candide* are rather sketchy, we must find the work's realism or "realism" in its portrayal of the human condition and in its attacks not only on fatuous Leibnizian-Panglossian optimism but also on religion, the wholesale slaughter of war, stubbornly held stupidities, and any number of other "civilized niceties." William F. Bottiglia speaks of, in *Candide*, "the central problem, that of human conduct in relation to the somber mystery of physical and social evil."[18] In *Candide* Voltaire makes much of the havoc, suffering, and death caused by the Lisbon earthquake, but natural disasters cannot be helped unless we choose to blame "God" or the "devil" for them. Bottiglia's "evil" is not the best term to employ because its opposite is "good," and a great deal of the so-called good in the world is not good at all, and many "good" people are hardly even alive. In the world there are a great many perverted people, vicious people, dangerous maniacs, et al., but if one is an astute student of character or of psychoanalysis mightn't that person ask Bottiglia if "social evil" is really all that mysterious? A far better statement than Bottiglia's is made by J. Robert Vignery vis-à-vis *Candide*: "At least equal to the existence of the regular clergy in its harmful effects upon the economy, declared Voltaire in *La Princesse de Babylone*, was war . . . ."[19] Alas, yes indeed. The enterprises of Jonathan Swift and Voltaire, like those of other great writers, are to correct and *unmask* man and to show mankind what in fact is the human condition.

[17.] "Gulliver's Fiction," *Studies in the Novel* 6 (1974): 8.
[18.] "Candide's Garden," *PMLA* 66 (1951): 718.
[19.] "Voltaire's Economic Ideas as Revealed in the *Romans* and *Contes*," *French Review*, 33 (1960): 262.

Both *Gulliver's Travels* and *Candide* can be considered to be *Bildungsromane*, or works in which the protagonist learns from his experiences. In the case of *Gulliver's Travels* there is the necessity of doing some hedging and saying that the learning is by and large *intermittent* if we choose to call it a *Bildungsroman*. Gulliver seems to learn most in his various visits in Book Three, in which he is an observer or reporter rather than an involved participant. *Candide*, is about as unqualifiedly good an example of a *Bildungsroman* as one could hope to find. For Candide learns from his experiences as the older Pangloss proves unable to do. Of course the fatuous Pangloss is Candide's teacher, and the "cheerio" optimism he learns from Pangloss he unlearns fast as before he leaves Europe he undergoes any number of awful experiences and even some disasters. And later in *Candide* he purportedly learns from his Manichaean friend Martin though Martin is so sketchily developed that for the most part he seems to be little more than Candide's travelling companion. Indeed, P. Cherchi says: "Anche Martin è abbastanza taciturno."[20] As to Pangloss Bottiglia says: "In each of these instances [cited above], Voltaire has Candide praise his former tutor, then contradict his philosophy."[21] There is little or nothing to praise in Pangloss, but note that Candide consistently contradicts him. Going a step further, Marc Bertrand says: "Candide, lui, ne semble être là que pour réfleter l'inanité de l'attitude panglossienne."[22] And most directly to the point Patrick Henry says: "*Candide* is a bildungsroman [sic] where the protagonist learns that the quest itself is futile . . . ."[23] Even as things are relatively clear in *Candide*, they are not as clear in *Gulliver's Travels*, as this Rawson statement attests:

> The tense hovering between laughter and something else, the structural indefiniteness of genre and the incessantly shifting status and function of the parodic element, the ironic twists and countertwists, and the endless flickering uncertainties of local effect suggest that one of Swift's most active satiric weapons [in *Gulliver's Travels*] is *bewilderment*.[24]

---

20. "Alcune note per un commento al *Candide*," *Zeitschrift für französische Sprache und Literatur* 78 (1968): 51.

21. *Voltaire's* Candide: *Analysis of a Classic*, Studies on Voltaire and the Eighteenth Century, vol. 7 (Genève: Institut et Musée Voltaire, Les Délices, 1959): 172.

22. "L'Amour et la sexualité dans *Candide*," *French Review* 37 (1964): 619.

23. "Time in *Candide*," *Studies in Short Fiction* 14 (1977): 87.

24. P. 17.

We know that *Gulliver's Travels* is a devastating assault on narcissism, but as Rawson points out, in all of its twists and turns there may well be bewidlderment often for Gulliver and sometimes even for the reader. And when Gulliver gets deeply involved in situations, as he is not in Book Three, he is not necessarily clearsighted. But Gulliver does learn some things from his experiences, and at the end of Book Four he has learned his lesson so well that he equates Yahoos, who are too like humans for our comfort, reductively with humans. On the other hand the Houyhnhnms have become his ideal to such an extent that on his return to England he spends much of his time in the stable with his horses. So in the end Gulliver has learned, albeit a bit reductively, that humans are Yahoos, and on the other hand there are any number of people in the world who, like Gulliver, have been driven daft by ideals. Wayne Burns's little book, *The Panzaic Principle*,[25] shows how the ideal is undercut and deflated in literary works by the realities in the work which hedge about the idealization, and this principle applies as readily to the hapless Pangloss as it does to Gulliver in the stable. So Gulliver has learned and also failed to learn, and, with the general exception of Book Three, if we are going to consider *Gulliver's Travels* as a *Bildungsroman*, we have to see it so with a kind of shatter effect, in bits and pieces and with insight alternating with obtuseness and not as the straightforward case we get in *Candide*.

Now we come to a topic as important as any in these works, even as important as satire, aggression primarily and anality secondarily. Anality does not figure prominently in *Candide* as such except in the form of aggression, for aggression is of course anal, and in *Candide* it is not really aggression so much as it is mayhem and wholesale slaughter, with some torture thrown in. In *Gulliver's Travels* there is some aggression and even warfare in Book One, but that, I think, a reader does not notice nearly as much as the aggression of the Yahoos in Book Four. For these humanoid creatures sometimes defecate on each other or pelt each other with excrement. But, filthy as they are, as far as I know they do not kill each other or other creatures (except for food) as the invading *Bulgares* do in *Candide*. And we have read history and know how often, and sometimes on extensive scales, humans have killed other humans. Aggression, whether it gets to the stage of open violence or not, comes about when people regress to the pre-Oedipal anal-sadistic stage. Of course aggressive people usually think that they are big, tough *hombres*, but, as we see, aggression is in fact *infantile*. It is a worst-scenario way of dealing with conflicts or problems with

---

[25.] (Vancouver, BC: Pendejo Press, n.d.) see passim.

people or of dealing with "innocent" people where negotiation, reasoning, gentle persuasion, or like means might far better be used. It is not only that aggression is anal, but it is also for other reasons that the lowly anus, a very neglected part of the human anatomy, needs serious attention. When one has an extra-good bowel movement and really gets cleaned out, a bowel movement is pleasurable. And Freud of course pointed out that the anal zone is an erogenous zone along with the oral and genital zones. But the anal zone, or the anus, has other undesirable functions besides eliciting aggression. The power urge is anal, and wretches in political-science departments go around whining "Power, power." And of course Freud pointed out that money is excrement, and far too many anally driven people, or perverts, live for money. Also, a good deal of human activity is in fact anal. Hotblooded people, if indeed they are hotblooded, are put to doing anal jobs. My scholarship is anal, but it is done to the end of liberating minds, and it is only in our minds that we can be free. As humans in various societies we can never be free, and everything we do is strictly determined or even overdetermined. Swift of course never reached the genital level and was fixated at the anal-erotic level,[26] and we have all heard how "Stella" and "Vanessa's" lives were ruined for love of Swift. It is not only the filthy Yahoos in *Gulliver's Travels* who are evidence of anality, but also so are the frequent mentions of Gulliver's "disburthening" himself. And when people urgently need to relieve themselves, bathroom functions can be an important part of life. But in *Gulliver's Travels* there are a number of psychopathic factors, for Milton Voigt sees in it "psychosexual infantilism, anal erotism, zoophilia, sodomy, exhibitionism, voyeurism, paraphilia, sado-masochism, guilt feelings, mysophilia, mysophobia, and compensatory potency reactions."[27] And Voigt also alludes to Phyllis Greenacre's noticing a "homosexual fellatio fantasy" vis-à-vis the monkey in Book Two.[28] Let us

---

[26.] See again the Brown Swift chapter passim. Swift's three poems on female anality, "Cassinus and Peter" (1731), "The Lady's Dressing Room" (1730), and "Strephon and Chloe" (1731), are utterly delightful. Often women like to announce that they have to urinate, but I infer that a good many women like to pretend they don't defecate, and some stupid people think female anality shouldn't be alluded to whereas women as well as men are filthy creatures.

[27.] "Swift and Psychoanalytic Criticism," *Western Humanities Review*, 16 (1962): 363. On infantilism in Book Two see Gerald J. Butler's unpublished essay, "Disturbed Oral Relationships and the Emotional Quality of Nourishment in Some Eighteenth-Century British Novels," p. 4. Also, see passim.

[28.] P. 364.

consider the Yahoos further. According to Gulliver the Yahoos "are cunning, malicious, treacherous, and revengeful."[29] Of course Gulliver, who idealizes the Houyhnhnms, is not necessarily the best observer of the Yahoos. But purportedly the Yahoos like shining stones, and so they are anal not only in their aggression but also in their avariciousness. This trait can be seen in that they devour everything. And of course they like nastiness and dirt. Female Yahoos in heat have an offensive smell. Gulliver is embraced by a female Yahoo, so the human-Yahoo link is exceedingly close.[30] The Yahoos are purportedly cowardly. And the Yahoos multiply like rabbits. Baudelairean spleen is often found among them. And Gulliver, according to the Houyhnhnms, is teachable, and the Yahoos are unteachable. So it would seem that the Yahoos are rather a "mixed bag," but at least they are very sexual and live very close to their unconsciousnesses, as humans do not. For humans it is important to study dreams as dreams are the royal road to the unconscious. John J. McManmon says: "Critics have often attempted to root the Fourth Book of *Gulliver's Travels* in Christian doctrine and morality."[31] The Houyhnhnms are no Christians, and the question of religion vis-à-vis the Houyhnhnms we shall get to in due time. Of course a few critics have called the Yahoos "sinners," and that is ridiculous both as a concept and in that the Yahoos have no conception of any morality at all. The Yahoos are aggressive, but James E. Gill rightly says of Yahoo wars that there is "much howling and very little real damage,"[32] which is a pleasant contrast to human wars. McManmon has brought up the subject, and John N. Morris says: "eschewing all subtlety, our author [presumably Swift] clearly establishes the yahoos as a Christ symbol, representing the church."[33] Well! I suppose it could be said that religious people are the most Yahoolike of all humans. And last, though much of this has been covered already, S. J. Sackett says: "men and Yahoos have many characteristics in common besides their physical appearance: both are quarrelsome, avaricious, gluttonous and

---

[29.] Citations from Swift in my text are to *Gulliver's Travels* in *Gulliver's Travels, A Tale of a Tub,* [and] *The Battle of the Books* (New York: The Modern Library, 1950). Here p. 302. A further page reference will be given in the text.

[30.] The best of Butler's poems I have seen is one about a female yahoo's love or lust for Gulliver.

[31.] "The Problem of a Religious Interpretation of Gulliver's Fourth Voyage," *Journal of the History of Ideas* 27 (1966): 59.

[32.] "Beast Over Man: Theriophilic Paradox in Gulliver's 'Voyage to the Country of the Houyhnhnms,'" *Studies in Philology,* 67 (1970): 544.

[33.] "Wishes for Horses: A Word for the Houyhnhnms," *Yale Review* 62 (1973): 191.

intemperate, politically corrupt, malcontented, lecherous, and gossipy."[34] Now we turn to *Candide*. We have noted Vignery's statement on the causes of war, both religious and economic. Bottiglia rightly speaks of "The horrific inhumanity and the brute senselessness of war . . . displayed in several chains of thematic fragments [in *Candide*] . . . ."[35] And indeed war is senseless and is destructive of much else besides human lives. Bertrand says: "Ce thème de la violence sexuelle est constamment mis en parallèle, dans *Candide*, avec d'autres exemples de violence: guerre, fanatisme, despotisme, anarchie."[36] Indeed in *Candide* there are many connections, and as to "anarchie" we must note that there is a difference between anarchy and anarchism and that anarchists love to organize. Anarchy is what we have now under the brutal and vicious reign of capitalism. And Roy S. Wolper makes this great statement: "Voltaire was aware of the close connection between stupidity and evil."[37] Of course warfare is stupid, "evil," and evidence that people have no awareness they are being anal. And stupid people, especially religious people, make a great deal of trouble in the world. I close with this statement made by Peter Fazziola:

> Candide's situation among the Bulgares can . . . be seen to reflect, in form of parody, Voltaire's view of [Blaise] Pascal's vision of man. Both have been chased from the earthly paradise, both find themselves imprisoned, both are forced to choose in a domain where they would rather not make a choice, and yet this choice has no bearing on whether or not they will be saved, for salvation depends entirely upon the will of the king, and of God in the other.[38]

---

34. "*Gulliver Four*: Here We Go Again," *Bulletin of the Rocky Mountain Modern Language Association* 27 (1973): 213. The following concerns the Houyhnhnms as well as the Yahoos, but note should be taken of this famous James L. Clifford statement: "By 'hard' [in Book Four] I mean an interpretation which stresses the shock and difficulty of the work, with almost tragic overtones, while by 'soft' I mean the tendency to find comic passages and compromise solutions." In his "Gulliver's Fourth Voyage: 'Hard' and 'Soft' Schools of Interpretations," in *Quick Springs of Sense: Studies in the Eighteenth Century*, ed. Larry S. Champion (Athens: U of Georgia Press, 1974) 33.
35. *Voltaire's* Candide, p. 198.
36. P. 624.
37. "Candide, Gull in the Garden?" *Eighteenth-Century Studies* 3 (1969): 272.
38. "Candide Among the Bulgares: A Parody of Pascal's *Pari*," *Philological Quarterly* 53 (1974): 433.

Pascal's "God" is of course entirely imaginary, and, chased out of Westphalia, Candide is set on his travels.

Now we come to the topic of utopias, or what may be taken as utopias, and "innocence." The reader can infer of course that the purported utopia in *Gulliver's Travels* is the little world of the Houyhnhnms. But what is the purported utopia in *Candide?* During his time in South America Candide visits the legendary Eldorado, and that is the supposed utopia in *Candide.* In Eldorado the people purportedly have nothing to ask "God" for, just things to thank "him" for. This little "paradise" is very isolated, but Candide and his valet Cacambo get in, and one would think that other people would get in and plunder and wreck Eldorado, but apparently this is not the case. And the isolation has a bad effect, for the people in Eldorado live in such a sublime "innocence" and "unanimity" that there is a lack of dialectic and (peaceful) disagreement and diversity. Voltaire does not idealize Eldorado, for Bottiglia says this: "Unreality, haziness, and parody are variously combined in the indications of incredible hugeness which Voltaire scatters through his depiction of the model society [Eldorado]."[39] Jean Sareil says: "Eldorado est d'abord une pause pour le lecteur quí accueille avec joie cet intermède statique après tant d'aventures échevelées. C'est aussi le moment le moins drôle du livre . . . . [40] Yes, Eldorado provides Candide and the reader with a chance to pause and rest, and indeed there Candide finds a static society, and the desideratum is a dynamic society. Ed Kelly seems to take a more positive view of Eldorado:

> The size, strength, and speed of the sheep are greatly exaggerated, as is everything in the Utopian Eldorado, but the very fact that Eldoradans have succeeded in training the proverbially dumbest of animals to do anything at all reasonable accentuates the accomplishments of a people undevoted to outer-world values.[41]

But it is unlikely that sheep can be trained to do anything except to gorge down food and to be still for shearing. And finally, William Mead says:

> El Dorado has proved very puzzling to a number of critics because it incorporates reforms that Voltaire himself is known to have longed for, such as tolerance, the achievement of deism,

---

[39.] *Voltaire's* Candide, p. 125.
[40.] *Essai sur* Candide (Genève: Droz, 1967) 56.
[41.] "The Obvious Meaning of Candide's Big Red Sheep," *American Notes and Queries* 9 (1970): 40.

the suppression of money, and the encouragement of learning. It has seemed hard to reconcile the presence of these elements with others, such as the isolation the country enjoys and the special nature of its soil, which plainly indicate that what is intended is a satire on Utopias.[42]

The Eldoradans' religion does not seem to me to be deism, and though deism is preferable to organized religion, it is yet religion and thus no achievement. The Houyhnhnm society has some positive features too, and that society we shall get to directly. But Mead is right to say that the society in Eldorado is satirized. The Yahoos have some negative traits, but at least they live in their bodies rather than in their minds and are close to their unconsciouses. The Houyhnhnms can see the Yahoos' negative traits, the Houyhnhnms have a "paranoid hatred" of the Yahoos,[43] and yet they are so "innocent" that the Master Horse is shocked by Gulliver's reports on England. Hence they are not especially aware. Furthermore, Knowles notes that "The limitations of Houyhnhnm society are often mentioned: its conformity, dullness, and joylessness."[44] And so here we encounter another static society. George Sherburn says: "In view of the evidence presented [above], the Houyhnhnms cannot be regarded as objects of satire."[45] So he, like Gulliver, idealizes the Houyhnhnms. James E. Ruoff corrects him by saying: "The Houyhnhnms are not in any sense ideal: Swift's view of life was too complex to admit of the romantic concept of absolute ideals."[46] Of course the Houyhnhnms are totally rational but also kindly and benevolent, and of course irrationalism at its worst can be dangerous. Many people complain that rationalism does not take account of emotion and feeling, but Freud was as rational as a man can be, and he has been wrongly accused of talking about nothing but sex. More recent rationalism has generally not been so insightful, for Herbert Marcuse aptly observed in the sixties, having in mind the technological world, that it was getting so rational it was in fact irrational, and of course it is far worse now. The critics spend far more time on the Houyhnhnms than on the Yahoos, and some critics, like Gulliver, idealize the Houyhnhnms,[47] but in fact Swift and his protagonist Gulliver

42. "Voltaire's 'Preromanticism,'" *Kentucky Romance Quarterly* 14 (1967): 145.
43. Ann Cline Kelly, "After Eden: Gulliver's (Linguistic) Travels," *ELH* 45 (1978): 47.
44. P. 135.
45. "Errors Concerning the Houyhnhnms," *Modern Philology* 56 (1958): 94.
46. "Swift's *Gulliver's Travels*, Part IV, Chapter III," *Explicator* 15 (1956): Item 20.
47. On "utopias" and ideals, see again Burns's *Panzaic Principle* passim.

spend far more time on the Houyhnhnms than on the Yahoos. There isn't space for me to cover all that has been said on the Houyhnhnms, who tend to enslave the Yahoos, but I'll quote two more critics in closing. William Bowman Piper records that "Claude Rawson has . . . acknowledged the strongly philosophical flavor of this voyage [Book Four]."[48] And of course the Houyhnhnms are articulate and rational as the Yahoos are not. But the topic of the philosophical I shall touch on briefly further on. And last Piper goes on to say that "The traditional notion is that humans are somewhat superior to Yahoos and somewhat inferior to the Houyhnhnms . . . ."[49] The "traditional notion" is mistaken, for the Houyhnhnms are too easy to idealize, and furthermore they are deficient in affect. And the Yahoos are in certain senses doubles of humans, and while they are very aggressive and have other negative traits (in common with many humans), they are more sexual and closer to their unconsciouses than nearly all humans, and it is only fostering human narcissism to think humans "superior" to Yahoos.

Our next topic is anxiety. And conveniently at hand is Gail Simon Reed's dissertation abstract, "Striving for Innocence: The Work of Anxiety in *Candide* and *Gulliver's Travels*."[50] Reed says:

> As counterpoise [from the "innocent self" facing "evil"], the narrator offers the reader a non-restricted vision by which he may observe the characters objectively and critically. Still, this more distant perspective does not preserve the reader from the disquieting verbal irony of *Candide*, one which forces the reader to face the unidealized and vulnerable aspects of himself, nor from the Dervish's equation of man with mice.[51]

And on *Gulliver's Travels* she says: "In *Gulliver's Travels* the narrator's defenses become the reader's."[52] And she concludes by saying: "Both in *Candide* and *Gulliver's Travels* anxiety-provoking material moves us away from narcissistic participation toward critical observation and thus makes us available for satire."[53] All well said, and what of particular instances? In Book One of *Gulliver's Travels*, in which Gulliver is huge and the Lilliputians tiny, the

---

[48] "Gulliver's Account of Houyhnhnmland as a Philosophical Treatise," in Smith, p. 181.
[49] P. 187.
[50] *DAI* 40 (1980): 4579A.
[51] 4579A.
[52] Again, 4579A.
[53] And again, 4579A.

Lilliputians experience great anxiety at the thought that feeding Gulliver may cause a famine. It is in Book Two, in Brobdingnag, that Gulliver experiences the most anxiety. For there he is tiny and the Brobdingnagians and all other living things huge. And it is when the Brobdingnagian monkey gets hold of him that Gulliver is in the most peril. At another time he has to kill giant rats with his hangar. And so on. But it is in Book Four that Gulliver faces the most interesting anxiety, for in Houyhnhnmland he is faced with the Yahoos and in Edmund Wilson's terms experiences the shock of recognition. In *Candide* it is mostly in the first third of the work, and secondarily in the second third, when he is in South America, that he is subjected to anxiety and even fear. The frightful folly of slaughter, torture, and mayhem in the first part would be enough to induce trauma in anyone. And it may be my repression-induced sadism, but I find it hilariously funny when an inquisitor beats Candide's buttocks in Portugal.

Next we come to fixed ideas. However accurate a person's ideas are, he or she has to recognize that reality changes (and a good many man-made changes only make things worse) and to recognize, with Fredrik Egerman in Ingmar Bergman's *Smiles of a Summer Night* (*Sommarnattens Leende*), that as one faces new situations, values have to be revised. To be fully functioning, a mind must be *flexible*. We have seen how Voltaire's Pangloss goes through all kinds of hell and still maintains fatuously and Leibnizianistically that this is the best of all possible worlds. He is even hanged and let down before he is killed[54] and still holds fast to his fixed idea. In Lilliput Gulliver sees obliquely and in flashes a little English society and system. Swift was careful not to press his point on this, and we need not equate Robert Walpole with Flimnap. But in Brobdingnag, where Gulliver is tiny, he brags about England to the king, fixedly assuming that England is just wonderful, and the king says rightly: "I cannot but conclude the bulk of your natives to be the most pernicious race of little odious vermin that nature ever suffered to crawl upon the surface of the earth" (p. 149). And we have seen how, after Gulliver experiences the Yahoos in Book Four, he revises his values and now has another fixed idea, that humans are Yahoos. And humans in fact are close cousins to Yahoos, but to equate humans and Yahoos is a bit reductive.

When I dealt with the realism of *Candide* and in *Gulliver's Travels* with the attempts of the narrator Gulliver to be realistic or "realistic," I of course

---

[54.] An incident still alluded to in Voltaire's time was the hanging of an Englishwoman, one Anne Greene, in 1650 and in which she was taken down and found to be still alive. On this see Charles Clay Doyle and Richard Ungar, "Dr. Pangloss and Anne Greene of Oxfordshire," *Romance Notes* 24 (1983): 174-75.

talked about the fantasy in *Gulliver's Travels*, all to the end of instructiveness or enlightenment. And what is fantastic in *Candide?* We have seen it already in Eldorado, for Eldorado is nothing more than an old myth, and of course utopias are desiderata and not actualities. We need not dwell long on this topic, but a little commentary is in order. For is Eldorado all that wonderful after all? David Fishelov says: "I would suggest that the true reason [for their leaving] lies in the fact that our two travelers [Candide and Cacambo], as well as Voltaire, are simply bored to death in Eldorado."[55] And indeed life in Eldorado is just static. Remarks on the fantasy in *Gulliver's Travels* are hard to come by, at least among the notes and quotations I have, but Voigt says: "Swift, like Sophocles, contributed a term—'Gulliver fantasies'—to psychoanalytic jargon, but Swift has been repaid with attentions which Sophocles has been spared."[56] It has even been held that everywhere he goes, Gulliver is in fact in England and seeing it in distorted ways.

If in fact Gulliver does travel, we are obliged to notice something. For Gulliver is a surgeon and could have found employment in England. And furthermore he is married and has children. And he leaves his wife and family and goes to sea; when he comes back at the end of Book Four, his wife and children are "loathesome Yahoos" and he cannot bear their stench. But then he stays in England writing his memoirs, having at the same time alienated himself from his wife and children. So we must conclude that Gulliver is a highly homoerotic man. And what in *Gulliver's Travels* is erotic? William R. Wray points out one very important thing:

> In Jonathan Swift's *Gulliver's Travels*, Book I, Chapter I, the pattern of Gulliver's references to his master, Mr. Bates . . . , seems to point to the probability of a sexual pun in the last reference of all . . . *Master Bates*. . . . That the sexual pun was intentional may further be suspected by the presence, in the key reference to Bates, of the words *dying* and *business*, both of which had sexual connotations for Swift and his contemporaries.[57]

Does Gulliver masturbate? We cannot know. And of course Swift's anal eroticism gets into *Gulliver's Travels*. We can infer that Gulliver has quite a bit of anal eroticism by his frequent references to his "disburthening"

[55.] "*Satura Contra Utopiam*: Satirical Distortions of Utopian Ideas," *Revue de Littérature Comparée* 67 (1995): 470. See this article also on *Gulliver's Travels* and George Orwell's *Animal Farm*.
[56.] P. 361.
[57.] "Swift's *Gulliver's Travels*, Book I, Chapter I," *Explicator* 26 (1967): Item 7.

himself. And it hardly needs mentioning that the Yahoos have a lot of anal eroticism, albeit some of it goes to aggressive and acquisitive ends. In Brobdingnag there is more "normal" eroticism as the maids of honor strip tiny Gulliver naked and lay him in their bosoms, and one girl even sets him on her nipples. In *Candide* we have seen that when Candide finally marries Cunégonde, she has become ugly and shrewish: rather a bad bargain. But also and among other things *Candide* is a love story, for from the start Candide loves Cunégonde, then beautiful, and he longs for her throughout much of the work. And he finds her a few times in the course of his travels. And in his travels he also encounters Pangloss. In life when a person leaves a locality and goes to another locality or other localities or to another country or other countries, he or she rarely encounters anyone from his or her original locality or country. But in fiction we tend to accept such improbable encounters. Again, among other things, *Candide* is a love story, but it is not a very erotic work. At random we can take this comment made by Bottiglia: "Candide's sentimental ideal holds firm until his final reunion with Cunégonde."[58] And that "final reunion" Panzaically undercuts his ideal of course. Even the most realistic lover is likely to overestimate his or her loved one.

Candide is rather short, but it is still too long to be a novella. Both it and *Gulliver's Travels* are in certain senses novels, but they are other things as well. *Gulliver's Travels* is also a satire, a travel book, a fantasy book, and perhaps there are other things it could be called. *Candide* of course is a satire and travel book as well, and we have seen that characterization is not Voltaire's forte, but *Candide* is also something else. And what is that? Bottiglia contradicts me as he says that *Candide* is a philosophical tale and not a novel,[59] and he has given us the clue. For in *Voltaire's* Candide he calls it a "*conte philosophique*,"[60] and indeed it is more that than a novel, and that generic classification perhaps in part explains why the characterization in it is so sketchy. At any rate, both *Candide* and *Gulliver's Travels* are multifaceted works.

Both *Gulliver's Travels* and *Candide* are parodic in a number of respects. Clifton Cherpack says of *Candide*: "From a literary standpoint, *Candide* is a parody, or, more precisely, a burlesque, since it mimics on a ridiculously low level a much more exalted kind of work."[61] And Catherine Cusset says further: "Parodie du roman sentimental, le conte [*Candide*] joue aussi à

---

58. *Voltaire's* Candide, p. 173.
59. "The Eldorado Episode in *Candide*," *PMLA* 73 (1958): 347.
60. P. 27.
61. "*Candide* as a Literary Form," in Waldinger, p. 39.

produire une double discordance, l'une dans les discours du héros, l'autre dans le contraste entre les corps et les désirs."[62] That it is a parody of sentimental novels would surely have been far more evident to eighteenth-century readers than it would be to twenty-first-century readers. But note that Bottiglia also sees this in *Candide*: "Brilliantly interwoven with the intellectual presentation of physical and social evil is the complementary assault on the sentimental foibles of the age."[63] We have been there before vis-à-vis Bottiglia and "evil," but his main point is well taken. And Bottiglia says in *Voltaire's* Candide that the "indications of incredible hugeness" in the depiction of Eldorado are, among other things, parodic.[64] And we saw earlier that Candide's situation among the *Bulgares* is a parody of Pascal's view of man. Thus we have established that *Candide* is a parody of sentimental novels and in places within it in other ways parodic. We have seen that Swift was steeped in travel literature, and it seems manifest that *Gulliver's Travels* is a parody of travel books, yet J. Paul Hunter asserts that "*Gulliver's Travels* has generally resisted efforts to consider it parodic . . . ."[65] But Piper speaks of "Gulliver's unconscious parody of Houyhnhnm reasoning . . . ."[66] And in fact vis-à-vis *Gulliver's Travels* Roger D. Lund does speak of Swift's "parody of travel narrative."[67] And also Lund says that "the mock explicitness and relentless circumstantiality of Gulliver's account" parodies conventions of the modern novel, as well as of travel narrative.[68] And Fishelov says *Gulliver's Travels* is both a satire and a parody of utopian ideals and ideas.[69] There is one thing more: Margaret Olofson Thickstun asserts that "Swift presents Gulliver's acceptance of Houyhnhnm reality as a parody of radical Protestant conversion experience."[70] Thus we see that *Gulliver's Travels*, like *Candide*, has a main parodic target, here travel narrative, as well as secondary targets.

[62] "Le Ridicule, arme mortelle?" *Infini* 25 (1989): 58.
[63] "Candide's Garden," p. 720.
[64] P. 125.
[65] "*Gulliver's Travels* and the Novel," in Smith, p. 65.
[66] P. 196.
[67] "Parody in *Gulliver's Travels*," in *Approaches to Teaching Swift's* Gulliver's Travels, ed. Edward J. Rielly (New York: Modern Language Association of America, 1988) 85.
[68] P. 84.
[69] P. 467.
[70] "The Puritan Origins of Gulliver's Religious Conversion in Houyhnhnmland," *Studies in English Literature, 1500-1900* 37 (1997): 519.

The next topic we can cover quickly because it has already come up under the rubrics of satire and aggression-anality and obliquely also in the discussion of other topics, and perhaps even to bring it up here is in large measure to belabor the obvious. For great literature, unless it is preeminently love-and-sex literature, nearly always deals with the failings or gross faults of a majority of humans, and even in love-and-sex literature there is often a measure of the inhumane. We have seen slaughter and mayhem in *Candide*, and not with just *Candide* in mind, it can be observed that violence is never an appropriate response to violence, and it is not only the human casualties of war but also the sheer destruction and ruin of entire economies. In *Gulliver's Travels* the target is preeminently human pretensions and narcissism, and if that were just a matter of people making asses of themselves, it would be rather comic, but "superior" people want to dominate and to subjugate "inferior" people, and even in these times slavery has not been altogether eradicated from the world. Furthermore, highly narcissistic people are so easily offended that they not infrequently become violent. And of course there are other targets in *Gulliver's Travels* and *Candide* besides narcissism and violence. There is a good deal in both on the sheer stupidity and lack of awareness of a majority of human beings, and of course in the fantasies Swift creates the commentary is always on humanity. And the Yahoos have their faults, but at least they live in their bodies, and it would be truly miraculous if the majority of human beings could accept their animality and just live in their bodies. When I am in my blackest moods, I am inclined to say that the human experiment has failed.

We have encountered the topic of the philosophical earlier, and in an important sense *Candide* is a lengthy philosophical debate between (fatuous) optimism and deepset pessimism. And Manichaeism, which sees life as a well-matched battle between forces of "good" and forces of "evil" and which is advocated by Martin in *Candide*, is somewhat more intelligent than the Christian view that "God" and "goodness" will ultimately prevail, and is more or less philosophical. And in *Gulliver's Travels* we have seen that the rational, rather dispassionate, and "innocent" Houyhnhnms tend to be philosophical. But as the Houyhnhnms don't engage in controversy and have no conception of the darker sides of experience, it is questionable how fruitfully philosophical they can be. And there is really no need to dwell further on these matters mentioned above, Book Three of *Gulliver's Travels* has been only touched on so far, and vis-à-vis this topic that book needs considerably more attention. As we all know, the seventeenth century effectively brought about the inception of modern science, but modern science was still in its early stages in Swift's time, "science" in Swift's time was neither necessarily wise nor right, and Robert C. Merton records that

Many of the "scientific" ideas that the Laputans expounded are ridiculous exaggerations of ideas and experiments that Swift might have read about in such journals as the *Philosophical Transactions* of the Royal Society. The way the flying island moved, for example, is largely an adaptation of Gilbert's theories of magnetism.[71]

And Robert P. Fitzgerald says that "A close reading of the description of the Struldbruggs suggests that Swift meant them to represent the [French] Academy, that he was writing in the tradition of satire and ridicule against it."[72] And, without going on the assault, Paul J. Korshin observes:

> In the broadest sense, the sources of the Flying Island include the entire history of man's attempts to fly by artificial or mechanical means before 1725, when Swift wrote Part III. But Swift scholars have narrowed the probable sources for Laputa to those in other philosophical or fantastic voyages: Lucian's *True History*, Cyrano de Bergerac's *Histoire Comique de la Lune*, and various mechanical contrivances provide known, though rather distant, analogues.[73]

Voltaire as well as Swift was influenced by Lucian, and both Voltaire and Swift were very fond of Rabelais.

Voltaire was such an outspoken opponent of all organized religion that many religious people undoubtedly consider Voltaire to be an incarnation of the "devil" and presumably conclude that he was an atheist, but in fact he was a deist, and deists, most of whom lived in the eighteenth century, of course believed in a clockmaker "God" who set the world in motion and then let it run of its own accord. And Swift of course was the Anglican dean of St. Patrick's Cathedral in Dublin, so both Voltaire, after a fashion, and Swift were religious men, but neither *Candide* nor *Gulliver's Travels* is in any important sense a religious work. And furthermore, Swift, fixated at the anal-erotic level, gives us sterling insights into the anality of humankind. Freud was well-read both in anthropology and in literature, I have now, I think, read everything Freud wrote except his letters, Freud said, "Ask the poets," and in that statement was of course alluding to

71. "The 'Motionless' Motion of Swift's Flying Island," *Journal of the History of Ideas* 27 (1966): 275.
72. "The Allegory of Luggnagg and the Struldbruggs in *Gulliver's Travels*," *Studies in Philology* 65 (1968): 661.
73. "The Intellectual Context of Swift's Flying Island," *Philological Quarterly* 50 (1971): 631.

other poets and writers besides William Blake and Novalis, I don't recall
Freud's having mentioned Swift, but Swift, the Anglican dean, with his
keen insights into human anality and character, was in fact a precursor of
Freud, whether Freud had read him or not. Voltaire, of course, was a figure
of the "Enlightenment," and Freud, although he was much influenced by
"romantic" poets, is often considered to be a latter-day "Enlightenment"
man, so in a sense there is also a link between Voltaire and Freud.

Voltaire, we have seen, was a deist, and as an "Enlightenment" man,
a determined pessimist, and, for example, a vigorous foe of the Catholic
Church and its dogmas, he was a very rational man. His Eldoradans cannot
be deists because they thank "God" for "his" supposititious goodnesses to
them, and so they are superstitious believers. Swift had strong misgivings
about rationalism, and although his Gulliver idealizes the rational
and "innocent" Houyhnhnms, it does not follow that his creator Swift
likewise idealizes them. But here we need to give more attention to the
Houyhnhnms. Knowles says: "Their [the Houyhnhnms'] moral philosophy
derives in large part from Stoic rationalism, which to some degree is echoed
in the rationalist Deism of the eighteenth century."[74] And Kathleen Williams
says: "The insistence on reason as a sufficient guide is of course the chief
characteristic of Deism, but many of the polemical Deists or freethinkers
were content to use it merely as an argument against Christianity . . . ."[75]
We note in the above two statements that no strong assertions are made
about rationalism and deism, but consider the following statement:

> [Irwin] Ehrenpreis is not alone in misunderstanding the
> Houyhnhnms, but I think he is the first to suggest the impossible
> notion that, in the Houyhnhnms, Swift is satirizing deism. To
> Ehrenpreis deists apparently are simply people who glorify
> reason.[76]

And of course some people who "glorify" reason are not deists but rather
atheists, I see nothing especially theistic about the Houyhnhnms, and I
tend to agree with Sherburn, the author of this last statement.

Novels or novelistic works can end in a variety of ways, but it is fairly
common, at least in earlier ones, that after having undergone adventures

---

74. P. 119.
75. "Animal Rationis Capax," in *Jonathan Swift's* Gulliver's Travels, ed. Harold
Bloom, Modern Critical Interpretations (New York: Chelsea House Publishers,
1986) 65.
76. Sherburn, p. 92.

and sometimes perilous experiences the protagonist returns home or now at last has a home and in some cases can live in peace and quiet. At the end of *Gulliver's Travels* Gulliver is apparently at home for good, and at the end of *Candide* Candide has a home, but neither really has peace and quiet, for Gulliver seems to be permanently deranged and disturbed, and Cunégonde, who was once a sweet and beautiful girl albeit she had her sexual wiles, has turned into an ugly and shrewish wife for Candide. But for both protagonists it is an ending in retreat. When he returns home, Gulliver busies himself with writing his memoirs, spends as much time as he can in the stable with his horses, and wants to have as little to do with his "Yahoo" wife and children as he can, which seems further evidence that he is highly homoerotic. And how does *Candide* end? It ends with Candide's famous statement: "mais il faut cultiver notre jardin" (p. 260). And why, in the end, does he decide simply to tend his garden? Wolper says that "The impulse to cultivate the garden is largely a result of Candide's visit with the old Turk . . . ."[77] That very well may be a precipitating cause, but it seems to me there are other causes as well. First, Voltaire was himself a gardener, Candide's garden is the seventh garden in *Candide*, and with such an author, what is more natural than that his protagonist be also a gardener? Second, having found himself married to an ugly shrew, Candide, I infer, expediently retreats to his garden and buries himself in gardening. Third, Karl Marx has pointed out how much modern work is alienated and alienating, but work which one chooses to do and even enjoys, and it is conceivably pleasant to tend one's own garden, can not only gratify a person but can also be a good way to sublimate. There are critics who think Candide's gardening stands for all sorts of activities, but gardening is essentially a very private activity in which, at most, the gardener may occasionally chat with his or her neighbors, Candide has learned well, especially in his initial experiences in Europe, that this is far from the best of possible worlds and that many humans are utterly vicious, and so it behooves him in the main to keep to himself and to tend his garden. It seems manifest to me that Voltaire is a pessimist and *Candide* a pessimistic work, but not all critics agree. For one, Rob Roy McGregor, Jr., asserts that "The Leibnitzian optimism which Voltaire wrote his story [*Candide*] to ridicule has the final word."[78] And my former professor, A[rthur] P. Stabler, responds thus: "It [McGregor's note] is saying, in effect, (1) that Candide went through an epic series of tribulations, (2) that his story has a happy ending, therefore (3) the

---

77. P. 268.

78. "Pangloss' Final Observation: An Ironic Flaw in Voltaire's *Candide*," *Romance Notes* 20 (1980): 364.

happy ending resulted from the tribulations," and further on Stabler says: "Candide's answer to Pangloss, then, rather than indicating that he misses the 'truth' of the latter's observation, shows that he and Voltaire are *denying its validity*."[79] Stabler wasn't one of my brighter professors, but in this controversy he is right on target. And, even granting that Candide gets some pleasure from his gardening, can we call it a happy ending when Candide is saddled with such a woman as Cunégonde has become?

I do not know that I have hit upon all possible ways to compare *Gulliver's Travels* and *Candide*, but I have manifestly done well. And of course I am not the first person to think of comparing the two. I have duly noted the Reed dissertation on anxiety in the two, Fishelov's "*Satura Contra Utopiam . . .*" discusses *Candide* and *Gulliver's Travels* as well as George Orwell's *Animal Farm*, and a few articles discuss both Swift and Voltaire. And there is yet another: Loy Otis Banks's short article, "Moral Perspective in *Gulliver's Travels* and *Candide*."[80] At first glance Banks's title may mislead a person in two respects. For his article is not a comparison of the two works but rather a series of contrasts. And despite the word "Moral" in the title, the article is refreshingly unmoralistic, but then the word is sometimes used to refer to the behavior of people or literary characters or to the attitudinal inclinations of authors or speakers. And as Banks provides contrasts of the two works and as there is a need to point out that *Gulliver's Travels* and *Candide*, similar as they are in a number of ways, in other ways are markedly different works, I shall conclude with a brief catalogue of some of the contrasts Banks notes. There is a major contrast in his first short paragraph:

> A reading of Swift's *Gulliver's Travels* and Voltaire's *Candide* . . . reveals several differences in moral perspective, perspective that is as different as the Saxon and the Gallic temperament. It is inconceivable that Swift could have written *Candide* and that Voltaire could have written *Gulliver's Travels*.[81]

Gulliver of course is English and very Saxon, and Swift was an Irishman who was not as sympathetic to his fellow countrymen as he might have been and who perhaps was as English as he was Irish. Banks also points out that Gulliver narrates his adventures whereas Candide is a third-person account,[82] and in fact it is hard to imagine Candide's being verbose or verbal enough to narrate his story. But Banks asserts that "Gulliver is an

---

79. "Voltaire Misses the Point?" *Romance Notes* 22 (1981): 124 and 125.
80. *Forum* [Houston] 4.7 (1965): 4-8.
81. P. 4.
82. Again, p. 4.

older and wiser man than Candide,"[83] and indeed Gulliver is older and has some experience, and Candide is very inexperienced at the start but learns quickly in the school of hard knocks whereas Gulliver is wiser in some situations than he is in others, he seems to be at his best in Book Three, and he is very inconsistent and overall not the wisest man. Banks is more accurate when he points out that circumstantially Gulliver is mostly alone whereas Candide usually has travelling companions.[84] Banks makes a more important distinction when he points out that Gulliver gets into situations where there is inferiority and superiority, real or supposititious, whereas Candide seems to encounter mostly dupes and knaves.[85] Last, Banks says that the narrative method of each, first person and omniscient, is suited to the subject matter, which well may be, but in his subsequent remarks Banks does not give Candide nearly the credit he deserves.[86]

A writer with a good understanding of human character, for example Jane Austen, can write tolerably well without necessarily having a keenly critical mind, but for a satirist keen critical powers are essential, bad satire is intolerably bad, and we can be grateful to Swift and Voltaire for having given us two such penetrating and great satires as *Gulliver's Travels* and *Candide*.[87]

---

83. P. 5.

84. P. 6.

85. Pp. 6-7. Note how conducive the "hierarchical" in *Gulliver's Travels* is to the generation of narcissism, Swift's main satiric target.

86. P. 8.

87. From its inception to its completion this essay has taken well over a year to do. I compiled over fifteen pages of bibliography on *Candide*, which was more than I needed, and a record thirty-three pages of bibliography on *Gulliver's Travels*, which was far too much. Needless to say, the process of researching all that bibliography required much time and labor, and when I got to the writing and documenting of the essay, I had, to borrow a term from library science, extreme problems with bibliographic control. In some cases I searched until I found just what I needed. In some other cases the documentation is "for-example" documentation, and considerably more might have been added. And in some cases what I had absorbed in the process of doing research, as it were by osmosis, gets into the essay undocumented. And the writing of the essay was interrupted by the process of moving from Pullman, Washington, to Eugene, Oregon, and getting set up in Eugene. I have worked both long and arduously on this essay, and at that it is neither my longest essay nor does it have a record number of endnotes, but it has been as difficult an essay to write as any I have done.

III

SEPARATIONS, ODYSSEYS, AND HAPPY ENDINGS:

TOM JONES AND *I PROMESSI SPOSI*

A ntonia Mazza raises the question as to whether or not Alessandro Manzoni, author of *I promessi sposi* [*The Betrothed*] (1821-42),[1] knew of and had read Henry Fielding's *Tom Jones* (1749), but she is unable to give an answer.[2] Unfortunately, little is known about Manzoni's early reading, and in the considerable Manzoni research I have done I find nothing which leads me to conclude that in fact he had read *Tom Jones*. Nonetheless, in

---

[1.] Some critics seem to think the definitive version of the novel was complete by 1840, but Bernard Wall, in *Alessandro Manzoni*, Studies in Modern European Literature and Thought (New Haven, Conn.: Yale U Press, 1954) 23, records that work on the novel began in 1821 and that the dates of the definitive edition are 1840-42. In its earliest form the novel was not *I promessi sposi* but rather was called *Fermo e Lucia*, and Andrea Ciotti, in "L'attesa di don Rodrigo e dell'Innominato, *Convivium* 28 (1960): 74, dates that early work not from 1821 but as done from 1820 to 1823. And in it the male protagonist's name is Fermo Spolino (see, for example, on this Renato Bertacchini, "La storia-rapina nei *Promessi sposi*," *Studium* 68 (1972): 546) and not Renzo or Lorenzo Tramaglino, but I assume the Lucia in it is Lucia Mondella, as she is in the later version. I haven't been able to see a copy of *Fermo e Lucia*, but from numerous critical remarks on it I know it is markedly inferior to *I promessi sposi*. Larry H. Peer, in "Schlegel, Christianity, and History: Manzoni's Theory of the Novel," *Comparative Literature Studies* 9 (1972): 276, is the only Manzoni critic I know of who states that there was an additional earlier version entitled *Gli promessi sposi*.

[2.] This question is raised in her "Coincidenze," *Vita e pensiero* 48 (1965): 9.

quite a number of ways *Tom Jones* and *I promessi sposi* are amazingly similar. At least one person before me has noticed the likeness of these two novels, for in her article "Coincidenze" ["Coincidences"], cited above in my second note, Mazza discusses quite a number of likenesses between the two novels. If she had seen all, or nearly all, the likenesses, there would be no point in my writing this essay, but in fact I have noticed quite a number of additional likenesses which Mazza didn't see or, if she did see them, didn't choose to discuss in print. And so, after covering the points Mazza makes, there being more ground to be covered, I shall proceed to discuss the other likenesses which I have noticed.

Three of Mazza's comparisons had not occurred to me although the second is so manifest in the novels I must have noticed it subliminally. First, she compares Fielding's Square and Manzoni's don Ferrante,[3] and indeed both are windbags. Second, in both novels she sees contrasts between the literary elements in them and the realities portrayed in them.[4] Because of Fielding's introductory chapters in *Tom Jones*, no intelligent reader of the novel could fail to see this contrast.[5] In *I promessi sposi* the literary elements don't exactly jump out at one as they do in *Tom Jones*, but they are evident enough. Manzoni's novel is historical, it is set in the seventeenth century, Manzoni obviously did a great deal of historical research preparatory to his writing of *I promessi sposi*, in the seventeenth century at least northern Italy was under Spanish control, and the novel is thick with texts, some in

---

[3.] P. 7. See also p. 8.

[4.] Again, p. 7.

[5.] And in *The Rise of the Novel: Studies in Defoe, Richardson, and Fielding* (Berkeley: U of California Press, 1965) 248, Ian Watt rightly points out that "Unlike Defoe and Richardson, Fielding was steeped in the classical tradition . . . ." Furthermore, in *Irony in* Tom Jones (University: U of Alabama Press, 1965) 91, Eleanor Newman Hutchens points out that "Classical literature provides Fielding [in *Tom Jones*] with numerous opportunities for referential irony." In "Fielding's Bill of Fare in *Tom Jones*," *Journal of English Literary History* 30 (1963): 237, Michael Bliss says: "The introductory chapters of *Tom Jones* are indeed an integral and organically functional part of the novel," but earlier he states (p. 235) that old-school critics concluded there was no relationship between these chapters and the fiction proper and that for modern critics these chapters pose a problem. I tend to agree with the old-school critics and would put my case in the following way. There were two Fieldings: (1) Fielding the great novelist, and (2) Fielding the magistrate, the public, "official" Fielding who tries to make Tom Jones prudent at the end of the novel.

Spanish, learning, and in addition don Abbondio's Latin.[6] Additionally, Manzoni has a supposed seventeenth-century anonymous source whom one knows to be fictitious because the anonymous source even gives reports on Manzoni's unhistorical protagonists, Renzo and Lucia. Manzoni did his homework admirably for the writing of *I promessi sposi*, but nonetheless Giovanni Titta Rosa asserts that Manzoni's seventeenth century is more Manzonian than historical.[7] The third and last is less a comparison than a striking coincidence, and it is noted by S. B[ernard] Chandler[8] as well as by Mazza.[9] In both novels exactly the same three lines from Shakespeare's *Julius Caesar* are quoted:

> Between the acting of a dreadful thing
> And the first motion, all the interim is
> Like a phantasma, or a hideous dream . . . .[10]

In *Tom Jones* these lines can be found in Book XV, Chapter iii, and in *I promessi sposi* they can be found in Chapter VII and are of course in Italian translation.

Anyone who saw the likeness of these two novels would not be able to miss the three main structural likenesses indicated in my title—the early separations of the lovers, the subsequent odysseys, and at the end the idealized happy marriages. Accordingly, it is strange that Mazza, who sees a number of less-noticeable likenesses, mentions these three main likenesses only obliquely. On the first she says only that the lovers initially can't marry.[11] In *I promessi sposi* this is manifest: don Rodrigo spots Lucia, sends a couple of his *bravi* or hired thugs to don Abbondio to forbid him

---

6. Of course Sir Walter Scott was the father of the historical novel, and Peer says (p. 279) that without Scott Manzoni couldn't have written *I promessi sposi* and that between 1819 and 1821 Manzoni read Scott's *Ivanhoe* and *Waverley*. But, strangely, Peer also records (p. 275) that Manzoni rejected the historical novel as a genre and furthermore (p. 279) that Manzoni even attacked historical novels!

7. "Storicita e fantasia dei *Promessi sposi,*" *Osservatore politico letterario* 8.1 (1962): 82.

8. In "A Shakespeare Quotation in Fielding and Manzoni," *Italica* 41 (1964): 323-25.

9. Pp. 6-7.

10. These lines are spoken by Brutus and occur in Act II, Scene i of the play. In *The Complete Works of Shakespeare*, ed. Hardin Craig (Chicago: Scott, Foresman, 1951), they can be found on p. 778.

11. P. 10.

to marry Lucia and Renzo, and of course the fearful don Abbondio refuses to marry them. In *Tom Jones* this factor requires a little explaining. Squire Western, Sophia's father, is initially very fond of Tom, but as Tom is held to be the bastard son of Jenny Jones, he wouldn't think of permitting Sophia to marry Tom. Only at the end, when Tom is discovered to be the bastard son of Bridget, Squire Allworthy's sister, will he allow and does he urge the marriage. Both in Somersetshire, where the novel begins, and in London, Sophia refuses to marry the loathsome Blifil despite her father's insistence and even entrapment. Tom and Sophia could run off and get married except for one thing: even loving Tom as she does, Sophia refuses to marry against her father's will. Second, Mazza mentions the "picaresca" ["picaresque"],[12] and this has to be an allusion to the odyssey sections of the two novels. The quintessential "picaresque" novel is Lesage's eighteenth-century *Gil Blas*. Otherwise, the concept is much overworked, but David Goldenopf calls the odyssey section of *Tom Jones* "picaresque" and sees this element as being somewhat at odds with Fielding's aims in the novel.[13] Last, Mazza's only remark on the endings of the novels is to say that Tom and Renzo are improved by Sophia and Lucia.[14] I have already pointed out that both marriages are idealized—and accordingly falsifying, and in subsequent remarks I shall expand on endings and on Mazza's rather dubious assertion here.

Mazza sees four more likenesses between the two novels. First, she sees in both an "aperatura umana" ["human opening"].[15] That is a bit too cryptic for me, but at any rate both novelists can be very human. When Fielding is not being his "official" self, when he is being a novelist, he is very human. Manzoni was deeply religious and intended *I promessi sposi* to be read as a religious novel, and of course much religious doctrine is inhuman, but in choosing as his protagonists two rustics or "rednecks," Renzo and Lucia, and in giving them his sympathies from start to finish, Manzoni shows that he too can be very human. And there has been some consternation among readers of the novel, especially early readers, because Manzoni chose rustics for his protagonists. Second, Mazza speaks of an "arguzia moralistica" ["moralistic keenness"][16] in both novels, and from that phrase I take it Mazza approves of moralizing and is perhaps a

---

[12.] Again, p. 10.
[13.] "The Failure of Plot in *Tom Jones*," *Criticism* 11 (1969): 265-66. See also p. 267.
[14.] Pp. 11-12.
[15.] P. 8.
[16.] Again, p. 8.

religious woman. We have seen that Manzoni was deeply religious, and the Marxist Gramsci holds that Manzoni's Catholicism caused him to repress his characters' historical individuality.[17] So what Manzoni couldn't have seen about *I promessi sposi* is that don Rodrigo, who wouldn't think of marrying Lucia but who longs to get into her panties or bloomers or whatever she wore and whom Manzoni apparently feels obliged to kill off, is his greatest character. And of course *Tom Jones* was also written with a moral aim. At the end, we note, Fielding wants us to believe that Tom has learned to be prudent,[18] but we also can see that Fielding isn't really shocked by Tom's "fornicating" and that, at least at Upton, he describes the "fornicating" with great gusto. And note that Kemp Malone, speaking of *Tom Jones*, says: "The sins of the flesh, such as sexual overindulgence and drunkenness, are taken lightly; it is the sins of the spirit which receive condemnation [e.g., those of Blifil, the totally anal calculating machine of a man] . . . ."[19] Third, in both novels Mazza sees an indulgent irony.[20] And indeed the title of an Eleanor Newman Hutchens book is *Irony in* Tom Jones,[21] and in that book she speaks of denotative, connotative, tonal, and referential irony.[22] Irony isn't employed quite as much in *I promessi sposi*, but it is nonetheless evident although in all the documentation I have on Manzoni criticism, Mazza's article is the only one I recall to mention his use of irony. The most obvious use of irony in *I promessi sposi* undoubtedly comes in Manzoni's treatment of don Abbondio. Irony has its uses in novels, but more remains to be said. At least in America irony has long been an English-department warhorse. Donn Rawlings has called irony the prevailing form of sentimentality, and Jerald Zaslove has said that irony is a way to hold off what is terrifying.[23]

[17.] In Robert S. Dombroski, "Manzoni on the Italian Left," *Annali d'Italianistica* 3 (1985): 101.

[18.] Gerald J. Butler, in *Henry Fielding and Lawrence's "Old Adam": A Reading of Restoration and Eighteenth-Century British Literature* (Lampeter, Wales: Edwin Mellen, 1992) 109, says: "Of course the anti-Tom is [the totally unsympathetic] Blifil. But Blifil also embodies the very 'morality' that Fielding thinks Tom should learn: Prudence." And note that Hutchens says (p. 101): "in *Tom Jones* the words 'prudence,' 'prudent,' and 'prudential' are used unfavorably three times to every one time they are used favorably."

[19.] "Fielding's *Tom Jones*," in *Literary Masterpieces of the World*, ed. Francis H. Horn (1953; rpt. Freeport, NY: Books for Libraries Press, 1968) 253.

[20.] P. 8.

[21.] For imprint information see note 5.

[22.] P. 68. See also pp. 69-99 and 119 passim.

[23.] Both these remarks were made years ago in conversation with me.

Last, Mazza sees a decided likeness between Sophia and Lucia,[24] and indeed both are extremely "nice," likeable girls. But what Mazza doesn't say is that the most notable likeness between them inheres in the novelists' treatment of the two girls, and in due time I shall discuss the novelists' treatment of them. And there are marked differences between the two girls. Gerald J. Butler is right to say that "In Sophia's . . . relation to Tom, she is in no way sexless, passive, or 'pure.'"[25] And Eléonore M. Zimmermann points out that "Timid Lucia trembles with terror at even a rough word from Renzo . . . ."[26] Furthermore, Richard H. Lansing rightly calls her "passive and submissive."[27] Undoubtedly, Lucia loves Renzo's body as well as his personality, but she is as religious as any character in the novel, including Fra Cristoforo and Cardinal-Archbishop Federigo Borromeo.[28] In fact, she even thinks she cannot marry after she vows to the "Virgin" Mary during her brief and terrifying abduction that if she is freed she won't marry. But of course Fra Cristoforo tells her that the "Virgin" wouldn't hold her to a vow made under duress. The only sign of real passion in her comes after her marriage, when she has numerous babies.

On a few points I am indebted to Mazza and also on one to Chandler, Mazza's article is rather short, and, again, if she saw more than what I have duly recorded from her article, she didn't choose to say more in print. There are quite a number of other likenesses between the two novels, and the greater part of the remainder of this essay will deal with them. First, Robert Scholes and Robert Kellogg say in their *The Nature of Narrative* that "The plot of *Tom Jones* . . . is essentially a Greek-romance plot . . . ."[29] And what exactly is a Greek-romance plot? They go on to say that

> The plot elements of these romances are highly stylized. A young couple fall in love, are prevented from consummating their love by various catastrophes which place them in grave danger while separated from one another, but they emerge chaste and unscathed, to marry at the end of the narrative.

[24.] P. 11.

[25.] P. 85.

[26.] "Structural Patterns in Manzoni's *I promessi sposi*," *Italica* 39 (1962): 170.

[27.] "Stylistic and Structural Duality in Manzoni's *I promessi sposi*," *Italica* 53 (1976): 358.

[28.] Borromeo was an actual historical figure and lived from 1564 to 1631. See on him D. M. White, "Manzoni and the Novel," *University of Leeds Review* 14 (1971): 129-30.

[29.] (London: Oxford U Press, 1966) 68.

Scholes and Kellogg go on to say that of course there were sometimes some exceptions in this pattern.[30] So we see that the separation, odyssey, and happy-ending pattern is an ancient one. That same plot over and over again in ancient Greece must have gotten monotonous. And we note that there were some exceptions in the pattern. For we have seen that Tom Jones "fornicates." But in *I promessi sposi* Renzo is a "good," repressed fellow, and both he and Lucia come to marriage "chaste," so *I promessi sposi* fits the Greek-romance pattern perfectly.

Both novels are quite long and exceedingly great novels. The edition of *I promessi sposi* I am using is about 540 pages of quite small print. The standard Wesleyan University Press edition of *Tom Jones*, which I am using, is two volumes and altogether about 980 pages of fairly large print. Leopold Damrosch, Jr., says: "The greatest single literary work of the eighteenth century is Fielding's *Tom Jones* . . . , that urbane and spacious fable in which pragmatic knowledge of the world is made to harmonize with gratified desire."[31] Numerous critics would agree with him, and surely some of them would call it the greatest English novel, but in my opinion Dicken's *Little Dorrit* is the greatest English novel. At various times I have read nearly all of the major eighteenth-century novels, English and continental, and I think *Tom Jones* and Jonathan Swift's novelistic *Gulliver's Travels* are the greatest eighteenth-century achievements, and of course *Gulliver's Travels* isn't nearly as long. Among Fielding's novels I prefer the dark *Amelia* and the satirical *Jonathan Wild* to *Tom Jones*, and I am fond of *Joseph Andrews*, and in that novel Lady Booby, who lusts after her servant Joseph, is my favorite Fielding character. I have no patience at all with religion, we have seen that Manzoni was deeply religious, but nonetheless I am fond of Manzoni and *I promessi sposi*. I have called *Tom Jones* one of the greatest eighteenth-century achievements but have also said that I prefer two other Fielding novels to *Tom Jones*, and in fact, for all its greatness, when I take *Tom Jones* not in part or parts but in toto, it is not a novel which I am particularly fond of. Archibald Colquhoun says:

> Few novelists have tried to concentrate as much into one book
> as Manzoni has in *I promessi sposi*. It is not only the first modern
> Italian novel; for Italy it is all Scott, Dickens, and Thackeray rolled

---

[30.] Again, p. 68.

[31.] "*Tom Jones* and the Farewell to Providential Fiction," in *Henry Fielding's* Tom Jones, ed. Harold Bloom, Modern Critical Interpretations (New York; New Haven, Conn.; Philadelphia: Chelsea House, 1987) 103.

into one volume; though it does not quite correspond to any of these, its spirit being perhaps nearer Tolstoy.[32]

Bernard Wall rightly says that Stendhal's *La Chartreuse de Parme* is the only other novel about Italy which ranks as high as *I promessi sposi*.[33] Indeed, there is broad general agreement that *I promessi sposi* is the greatest Italian novel, I have read widely in the Italian novel, and I share that view. In my opinion the second-greatest Italian novel is Giovanni Verga's *Mastro-don Gesualdo*, available in English under that title in a D. H. Lawrence translation. And I think Elio Vittorini's *Conversazione in Sicilia* [*Conversations in Sicily*] is the third-greatest Italian novel. Also, Alberto Moravia is vastly overrated, but his *Il conformista* [*The Conformist*] is a very fine novel, and the Bertolucci film version of that novel is splendid. And Verga's *I malavoglia* [*The House by the Medlar Tree*] is a very fine novel, and in Mikhail Bakhtin's terms it is a polyphonic novel. Manzoni lived a very long life, from 1785 to 1873. We have seen that Fielding published other fine novels besides *Tom Jones*. And *Tom Jones* is a very great and very long novel, but Fielding got it done in a four- or five-year period, for it was published in 1749, and in it there are numerous mentions of the 1745 Jacobite rebellion. And *I promessi sposi* is the only novel that Manzoni wrote; his other publications are plays, poems, and religious homilies. He lived a long life and had time to write another novel or other novels unless his later years were unduly hectic, beset by financial crises, etc. But we have seen that it took Manzoni over twenty years to get out the definitive version of *I promessi sposi*, and if he had written another novel or two, he most likely would have felt obliged to spend years on it or them, and at that, had he written another novel or two, it is extremely unlikely he could have written anything to equal *I promessi sposi*.

There are quite a number of things wrong with Dickens's early novels, but after the completion of *Martin Chuzzlewit* he planned all his novels very carefully, and a number of his later novels are over eight hundred pages long. *Great Expectations* is not one of Dickens's longest later novels, it being not quite five hundred pages long, but it is his most nearly perfect novel. The criticism I have read on *Great Expectations* has been mostly

---

32. "Alessandro Manzoni," in Manzoni's *The Betrothed*, trans. Colquhoun (New York: Dutton, 1961, c 1951) 606. Colquhoun's is the best translation of *I promessi sposi* into English. The next-best translation into English is by Bruce Penman, but that is less literally accurate than Colquhoun's. On both and the reception of *I promessi sposi* in Britain and America see Augustus Pallotta, "British and American Translations of *I promessi sposi*," *Italica* 50 (1973): 483-523 passim.
33. P. 51.

laudatory, and critics can find very few things to complain about in it. We have seen that *Tom Jones* and *I promessi sposi* are by general agreement very great novels, but neither novel is nearly perfect. In my view the major thing wrong with *Tom Jones* is something for which numerous critics have praised the novel, its elaborately constructed plot. The most famous and most laudatory statement on the novel's plot was made by Samuel Taylor Coleridge: "Upon my word, I think the *Oedipus Tyrannus* [of Sophocles], *The Alchemist* [of Ben Jonson], and *Tom Jones*, the three most perfect plots ever planned."[34] *Tom Jones* is a very symmetrical novel. The first six books take place in Somersetshire, then come six odyssey books, and the last six books take place in London except at the very end the main characters are back in Somersetshire. The first six books are carefully plotted, but in them plot is not so excessive that it becomes obtrusive. Fielding obviously intended *Tom Jones* to be carefully structured and plotted, and Goldenopf has pointed out that the "picaresque" odyssey books are so loosely structured and episodic that they are at odds with Fielding's aims in the novel.[35] But I, for one, have no complaints about the episodic nature of the odyssey books. In sharp contrast to the looseness of the odyssey books, the last, London books are so plotted that there is little in them but plot, and the reader is hard put to keep all the twists and turns of the plot straight. The London books, in my view, are the main thing wrong with *Tom Jones*. In them one has to wade through Nightingale's troubles with women and his father, the machinations of the lawyer Dowling, etc., and then when things look worst for both Tom and Sophia, things so swiftly and almost miraculously get better for them that they lead to an idealized happy ending back in Somersetshire. In my view the best things in the London books are the portraits of two urban, "noble" decadents, Lady Bellaston and Lord Fellamar. There are also a few problems in characterization in *Tom Jones*. All the characters in the novel except three are very alive, human, and three-dimensional, and the problem with Sophia is not in Sophia herself but in Fielding's treatment of her, which I shall discuss in tandem with Manzoni's treatment of Lucia. But who then are the three exceptions? They are Thwackum, Square, and Squire Allworthy. Fielding attempts to endow Thwackum and Square with emotions, for both are said to want to marry Bridget, Squire Allworthy's sister, and he endows each with a very human trait, for Tom finds Square hiding in Molly Seagrim's

---

[34]   From his *Table Talk*, 5 July 1834 (new ed., 1905) and quoted in *Henry Fielding*, ed. Claude Rawson, Penguin Critical Anthologies (Harmondsworth, Engl.: Penguin, 1973) 259.

[35]   See again pp. 265-66.

closet, and of course Thwackum is a sadist, and that is a pervertedly human trait. But all in all Thwackum and Square are little more than mutually antagonistic positions. Square is a deist and is inclined to be optimistic about man and nature. Thwackum is a fundamentalist before the time of fundamentalists and holds that mankind is totally evil and that the only hope for mankind is "grace." And in the novel these two seem to exist mainly to tear into each other.[36] Perhaps a large part of the problem with Squire Allworthy is that he was modelled after Fielding's benefactor, Ralph Allen.[37] Arnold Kettle says: "Allworthy is almost an allegorical figure, scarcely individualized at all . . . ."[38] And Butler says: "We can only take him [Allworthy] seriously because we are in effect *told* to do so by Fielding . . . ."[39] Allworthy is all "goodness," but even more bothersome to me than his "goodness" is that he, a mature man, is such an innocent. He is in fact such an innocent that he misjudges Tom, who can get into trouble, and turns him out. And he keeps Blifil, whom he should have seen was nothing but an anal calculating machine, but of course Blifil is a kind of house pet who avoids getting into trouble, and his "sins" are known to Allworthy only at the end of the novel. Fielding was opposed to Samuel Richardson in everything, and his consequent deliberate limitations on *Tom Jones* have been the cause of some adverse criticism, but this is a topic I shall deal with when I get to Fielding's differences from Manzoni. Manzoni intended *I promessi sposi* to be read as a religious novel, and Larry H. Peer rightly says that the conversion of the "criminal" Innominato [the Unnamed One] is the most disputed thing in the novel.[40] And as the Innominato has had his *bravi* abduct Lucia, his timely conversion is nothing short of "providential." The Innominato was modelled after an

---

36. Nonetheless, inadequate as they are, J. Paul Hunter, in *Occasional Form: Henry Fielding and the Chains of Circumstance* (Baltimore: Johns Hopkins U Press, 1975) 125 and 126, asserts that Square was modelled after one Thomas Chubb and Thwackum after one Richard Hele.
37. William Empson, "*Tom Jones*," *Kenyon Review* 20 (1958): 223 and Allen was one "whom Fielding would be ashamed to laugh at" (also p. 223).
38. "*Tom Jones*," in *Henry Fielding und der englische Roman des 18. Jahrhunderts*, ed. Wolfgang Iser, Wege der Forschung, Bd. CLXI (Darmstadt: Wissenschaftliche Buchgesellschaft, 1972) 42, and in the same sentence Kettle says: "Square and Thwackum are like ninepins, put up in order to be knocked down."
39. *Fielding's Unruly Novels*, Salzburg Series (Lampeter, Wales: Edwin Mellen, 1995) 109.
40. P. 277.

historical Conte del Sagrato,[41] and Chandler asserts that he, obviously in his "criminal" phase, derives from the *Sturm und Drang*.[42] It was of course don Rodrigo who had the Innominato abduct Lucia, and purportedly even beforehand the Innominato was having misgivings but took on the job to save face. He holds the terrified Lucia overnight, supposedly experiences his conversion, and releases her the next day. And thereafter he is supposed to be all "grace" and lovingkindness. His conversion is incredible, and I can think of only one possible explanation for it. We cannot know whether or not the Innominato had religious training as a child, but from flashbacks in Federico Fellini's films *Otto e mezzo* [*8 1/2*] and *Giulietta degli spiriti* [*Juliet of the Spirits*] we know how rigorous and even traumatic Italian Catholic training in childhood can be. And even in an enlightened adulthood, rigorous childhood religious training can come back to haunt the adult and even distort the adult's thinking. And the only possible explanation I can see for this conversion is that childhood religious drilling came back and so haunted the Innominato and made him feel so guilty he was converted. But of course we know nothing at all about his childhood, so this possible explanation is sheer speculation. We have seen that Manzoni intended *I promessi sposi* to be read as a religious novel, and so it is easy to infer that, as well as the unlikely transformation in the Innominato, there are problems in the novel with various very "good" characters. There is indeed some idealization in the novel. But aside from the improbable conversion of the Innominato, the other main problem with *I promessi sposi* inheres in the conflict between the religiosity in it and other currents or forces in it. Vittorio Spinazzola says:

> *I promessi sposi* approdano dunque a una profonda contraddizione: da un lato l'energico impulso operativo, la volontà di intervenire fattivamente sulla propria epoca, l'appello agli italiani perché prendano in mano il loro destino e lo risollevino, restituendo a miglior sorte il paese; dall'altro lo sconsolato pessimismo sulli reali facoltà dell'uomo, incapace, anche se sorretto dalla piu fervide fede, di modificare durevolmente il caos delle cose terrene.[43]

[41.] Pallotta, "Characterization Through Understatement: A Study of Manzoni's Don Rodrigo," *Italica* 58 (1981): 44.

[42.] "Passion, Reason and Evil in the Works of Alessandro Manzoni," *Italica* 50 (1973): 562.

[43.] "La contraddizione dei *Promessi sposi*," *Acme* 22 (1969): 30.

[*I promessi sposi* comes thus to a deep contradiction: on the one hand the energetic operative impulse, the will to intervene in fact in one's own era, the call to the Italians to take in hand their own destiny and to elevate it, restoring the country to a better state; on the other hand the disconsolate pessimism about the actual faculties of man, incapable, thus sustaining himself with the most fervid faith, in order to modify durably the chaos of earthly affairs.]

We have seen that at least the northern Italy of the time of the novel was under Spanish control, and northern Italy at the time the novel was written was under Austrian control and must have been strongly irredentist. But of course Spinazzola's main point is the contradiction between the liberal, progressive historicism of the novel and its religious pessimism. Questions have been raised about just how liberal Manzoni was,[44] but at any rate Manzoni's sympathies are all with the little people, and about the only one of the high and mighty in the novel who is presented positively is the historical figure Borromeo who, as Manzoni presents him, is such a Christian in the best sense of the word that he even concerns himself about "lowly" people. The contradiction Spinazzola points out is indeed there and is a major flaw in the novel, but at that it creates an interesting dialectical interplay or tension in the novel between liberal progressive impulses and pessimism about mankind in general. We may realize that the human situation and the way most people are are hopeless, but we still have urges to try to do something.

Both *Tom Jones* and *I promessi sposi* are novels in which there is considerable action, and they could even be considered "adventure" novels. This is particularly true of their odyssey sections. We have seen that Lucia experiences a brief and terrifying abduction. And after Renzo is arrested in Milan in the morning at the inn, he addresses the crowd in the street thus: "'figliuoli! me menano in prigione, perchè ieri ho gridato: pane e giustitia. Non ho fatto nulla; son galantuomo: aiutatemi, non m'abbandonate, figliuoli!'"[45] ["'Sons! they are taking me to prison, because yesterday I shouted "Bread and justice." I have done nothing wrong; I am an honest man: help me, don't abandon me, sons!'"] We see that Renzo mentions the word "pane" ["bread"]. And indeed there had been a terrible harvest, and there were bread riots in

---

44. See, for example, Spinazzola, p. 38, and Titta Rosa, pp. 86-87.

45. Citations from Manzoni in my text are to *I promessi sposi*, introduzione e note di Vittorio Spinazzola ([N.p.]: Garzanti, 1966). Here Ch. XV (p. 219). Further references will be given in the text.

Milan when Renzo arrived, but of course he wasn't arrested for rioting. At any rate the crowd frees Renzo, and he flees out of the city and journeys to Bergamo, where his cousin Bortolo finds work for him. And as Bergamo is under Venetian jurisdiction,[46] there Renzo is free from prosecution. But Renzo is not forgotten in Milan, and as he addressed the crowd and the crowd released him, he is held to have started a riot. So after a time it becomes too hot for him even in Bergamo, and he has to move elsewhere and live under the assumed name of Antonio Rivolta. Carol Lazzaro-Weis holds that to call *I promessi sposi* a "*roman d'aventures*" is "unfitting" and "too restrictive,"[47] but even at the start of the novel there is vigorous action, and in large measure it is a novel of action. And unlike Richardson's *Clarissa Tom Jones* is a novel of action. The greatest thing in *Tom Jones* is the sequence of events at the inn at Upton. There are frequent and hilarious fights there, Tom "fornicates" there with Mrs. Waters, Sophia arrives just in time to learn that Tom is in bed with Mrs. Waters and leaves her muff for Tom,[48] and Fitzpatrick, hot in pursuit of his estranged wife, arrives and, thinking Tom is in bed with his wife, bursts into the room where Tom is in bed with Mrs. Waters and fights with Tom. And from the events at Upton I infer that Fielding had a rather low opinion of innkeepers. And of course also there is quite a bit of action in the first and last parts of the novel.

Mazza and Chandler have pointed out the amazing coincidence of the same three lines from Shakespeare's *Julius Caesar* being quoted in *Tom Jones* and *I promessi sposi*, and of course a brief quotation in each doesn't mean significant influence, but in fact both Fielding and Manzoni were influenced by Shakespeare—and by Cervantes as well. Manzoni saw in Shakespeare a "moral reality,"[49] and indeed in Shakespeare's plays there are

---

46. Markus Lakebrink, "Manzonis *I promessi sposi* in literatursoziologischer Sicht," *Germanisch-Romanische Monatsschrift* [neue Folge] 32 (1982): 195.
47. "The Providential Trap: Some Remarks on Fictional Strategies in *I promessi sposi*," *Stanford Italian Review* 4.1 (1985): 96.
48. Muffs are open at both ends, so they are unavoidably suggestive of vulvas. And most muffs are furry, so they are also suggestive of pubic hair. In his very thorough note, "The Device of Sophia's Muff in *Tom Jones*," *Modern Language Notes* 74 (1959): 685-90, Maurice Johnson notes the muff's function vis-à-vis physical attraction between Tom and Sophia (p. 685) and even notes that Sophia takes the muff to bed with her (p. 689), but he fails to mention the genital significance. But Emily A. Hipchen, in "Fielding's *Tom Jones*," *Explicator* 53.1 (1994): 16, says: "By the early eighteenth-century [sic], *muff* had acquired its now current usage as a vulgarism for the female genitalia . . . ."
49. Peer, p. 272.

any number of "moral" issues, but I take it Manzoni didn't know *Measure for Measure*, Shakespeare's most sexual and "immoral" play. And in Manzoni's sometimes richly vivid characterization the influence of Shakespeare is inferable. Daniel Defoe and Richardson were not especially learned men, but Fielding was steeped in the classical tradition and undoubtedly also in English literature. In all the documentation I have on Fielding the only mention of Shakespeare I can find is vis-à-vis the *Julius Caesar* quotation, but in creating his rich panorama of characters in *Tom Jones* and his other novels, I infer that he was influenced by Shakespeare, and especially by Shakespeare's comedies. There is quite a bit of action in Shakespeare's plays, but of course there is in them mainly dialogue, and Fielding and Manzoni were novelists. Cervantes' *Don Quijote* was the second great novel to be written in the West after Rabelais' *Gargantua et Pantagruel*, and it is of course not only early but also one of the greatest and most influential of Western novels, and both Fielding and Manzoni were more influenced by Cervantes than by Shakespeare. We have seen that at least northern Italy was under Spanish domination in the seventeenth century, and there is quite a bit of Spanish in *I promessi sposi*, albeit not always the best Spanish. And Manzoni was not only versed in the Spanish language but also in Spanish literature, as is attested by Giovanni Getto's extremely long article, "*I promessi sposi*, i drammaturghi spagnoli e Cervantes"[50] ["*I promessi sposi*, the Spanish Dramatists, and Cervantes"]. Getto points out that Manzoni knew a number of Calderon and Lope de Vega plays,[51] and he makes several useful comments vis-à-vis Cervantes. Manzoni has a supposititious seventeenth-century source, and in *Don Quijote* Cervantes claims to have an Arabic source.[52] A number of stories are told in *Don Quijote*, and Getto sees a likeness between Cervantes' Lucinda and Lucia.[53] Perhaps Getto's best point is that don Abbondio and his calmer, more sensible housekeeper Perpetua are analogous to Don Quijote and Sancho Panza.[54] And I don't recall Getto's having mentioned Cervantes' delightful *Novelas ejemplares*, but Enzo Noè Girardi sees a considerable influence of this work on *I promessi sposi*.[55] Fielding mentions Don Quijote at least once in *Tom Jones* and possibly more times. Henry Knight Miller says:

[50.] *Lettere italiane* 22 (1970): 425-99.
[51.] P. 499.
[52.] Getto, p. 484.
[53.] P. 492.
[54.] P. 490.
[55.] "Manzoni e Cervantes," *Aevum* 37 (1963): 543-52 passim.

> Henry Fielding may very well have been seeking . . . to identify his own prose romances with the dignity of the highest poetic kind by calling them Comic *Epics* in Prose; but, in following Cervantes (or at least the Canon of Toledo) who . . . had declared that the epic could be written in prose, he was primarily acknowledging that this was the most important *narrative* model that was at once familiar to his audience and of unquestioned major stature as literature, as he could not escape knowing his own work was.[56]

It is probably questionable to call Fielding's novels "romances," but we must keep this statement in mind when we get to the topic of epic qualities. The thing in it most to our purpose here is the acknowledgment that Fielding followed Cervantes (and his Canon). And we must cite Miller again, for elsewhere he says:

> The second "interpolated tale" of importance in Tom Jones [sic] is that which Mrs. Fitzpatrick tells—with several of those hurly-burly interruptions such as constantly intrude upon the "digressive" narratives of *Don Quixote* [the first "interpolated tale" in *Tom Jones* is that of the Man of the Hill].[57]

And of course it is not only the interruptions in them but also the fact that, as in *Don Quijote*, there are "interpolated tales." Manzoni doesn't precisely include "interpolated tales" in *I promessi sposi*, but there are in it nonetheless a number of digressive narratives which may owe something to Cervantes' digressions. As to Fielding, I think anyone who knows both *Don Quijote* and *Tom Jones* would see more indebtedness on Fielding's part than just to Cervantes' Canon and to the digressive narratives and their character.

Both *Tom Jones* and *I promessi sposi* are novels which have narrators. Critics most often like to make sharp distinctions between author and narrator, in effect denying that the author or novelist or storyteller is the narrator. In some cases there are indeed distinctions: in Dickens's *Great Expectations* the narrator is not Dickens but rather the adult Pip, and in Franz Kafka's story "Ein Hungerkünstler" the narrator is several cuts below Kafka's level of sensitivity. But as the critics have gone on endlessly on this topic, I, in

---

[56] *Henry Fielding's* Tom Jones *and the Romance Tradition*, English Literary Studies, ELS Monograph Series No. 6 (Victoria, BC: U of Victoria, 1976) 8.

[57] "The 'Digressive' Tales in Fielding's *Tom Jones* and the Perspective of Romance," *Philological Quarterly* 54 (1975): 264.

my reading and rereading, have in most cases concluded that author and narrator were indeed one and the same. And in the cases of *Tom Jones* and *I promessi sposi*, whatever Fielding and Manzoni critics may have concluded on the matter, I hold that the narrators are indeed Fielding and Manzoni, and the fact that their narrators seem to have the full range of Fielding's and Manzoni's learning makes me rest easy in my conclusion.

Don Rodrigo's *bravi* break into the homes of Renzo and Lucia when they are elsewhere in the village, friends inform them, fortunately Fra Cristoforo is there and makes arrangements for them, and Renzo and Lucia have to flee from the village. Lucia's mother, Agnese, leaves with them but returns home after a time. Lucia is at the convent at Monza until her abduction, and after she is released, she lives quietly in Milan with don Ferrante and his wife, donna Prassede. We have seen that Renzo is overnight in Milan and has to flee from the city. At the time of the plague he comes back to Milan and locates Lucia, recovering from the plague, in the *lazzaretto* or makeshift hospital by recognizing her voice. And we have seen that Tom and Sophia are from Somersetshire and that near the end of *Tom Jones* they are in London for a considerable time. So in both novels there is a country-city contrast. When Sophia leaves home, she does in fact end up following Tom, but it is important to note that she leaves home not to follow Tom but rather to escape from a forced marriage to Blifil. She heads for London, knowing that in London she can stay with Lady Bellaston. As she has a contact in London, perhaps she has been in London before. And I see no evidence that Tom, Renzo, and Lucia have ever been in a city before they get to London and Milan. Lucia lives for a considerable time in Milan with an aristocratic couple who shelter and protect her, and perhaps she does little going out and exploring Milan. In Renzo's initial, brief, and traumatic time in Milan he may have gained considerably more experience of the city than Lucia ever did. Tom is raised as the foster son of Squire Allworthy, a country gentleman, and he got such education as Thwackum and Square could provide. In his Somersetshire environment there seem to be a fair variety of people. Renzo and Lucia may never have gone far out of their village before they have to flee, Renzo can't read very well, he and Agnese have to have people write letters for them, they had no access to don Rodrigo's residence, and perhaps at the start of the novel the only educated people Renzo and Lucia had ever met were don Abbondio and Fra Cristoforo. Some rather shrewd people sometimes wonder if the differences between country life and city life are really so great. If Sophia, a squire's daughter and so country "gentry," had been in London before, it was likely for a brief visit or visits. Having in mind their more privileged backgrounds and the question as to whether country and city are really so different, I infer that Tom and Sophia may not have gained all that much from their time in London. But the rustics or "rednecks" Renzo and Lucia, who at the start of *I promessi sposi* probably knew only other rustics as well as don Abbondio and Fra Cristoforo, would seem to stand to gain by their experiences of city life. But aside from what she experienced during her brief and terrifying abduction, there is a real question as to how much more experienced Lucia is at the end of the novel. On the contrary, at the end of the novel Renzo is considerably more experienced than he was at the start of the novel, but of course all that experience was not gained in Milan. After the marriage is prevented, Agnese sends Renzo to a lawyer named Azzecagarbugli to try to get help, on his entry into Milan Renzo seems to enjoy the excitement of the bread riots, and Gregory L. Lucente correctly points out that both with the lawyer and in Milan after the bread riots Renzo is out of his element.[58] Making a different point about Renzo's experience of Milan, Ezio Raimondi says:

> Perché anche Renzo prenda a riflettere a sua volta su quanto gli è successo, occorre aspettare che egli entri a Milano e che i nuovi eventi di cui è spettatore o compartecipe lo portino ripetutamente a un confronto, a un dialogo con i propri ricordi, che poi è forse anche, sul piano dell'arte, una delle grandi scoperte manzoniane.[59]

> [Because Renzo also begins to reflect in turn on what has happened to him, we can expect that when he enters Milan and when the new events of which he is a spectator or in which he is a participant lead him to a confrontation, to a dialogue with his memories, which is also, in the sphere of art, one of the great Manzonian discoveries.]

And indeed Milan is a discovery for Renzo. Robert S. Dombroski says: "Truth, for his [Manzoni's] characters, exists prior to experience. (Those who, like Don Abbondio, presume that experience can dictate a code or system . . . receive from their author an ironical smile of disbelief.)"[60] Whatever we may think of don Abbondio, it is obvious that a person or character who thinks truth is prior to experience is likely to experience

---

[58.] "The Uses and the Ends of Discourse in *I promessi sposi*: Manzoni's Narrator, His Characters, and Their Author," *Modern Language Notes* 101 (1986): 55.

[59.] "*I promessi sposi* e la ricerca della giustizia," *Modern Language Notes* 83 (1968): 7.

[60.] "The Seicento as Strategy: 'Providence' and the 'Bourgeois' in *I promessi sposi*," *Modern Language Notes* 91 (1976): 87.

some disasters. But Dombroski also points out that by the end of the novel Renzo has learned that truth is gained from experience.[61] Charles A. Knight says: "At the outset Fielding describes the clear structure of the novel [*Tom Jones*] in terms of basic locale and its moral implications: . . . [a] Horatian country-city antithesis . . . ."[62] Indeed, Tom and Sophia learn a fair amount in London, but Renzo, who spends the least time in the city, learns more than Tom, Sophia, and Lucia.

Both novels are in certain respects *Bildungsromane.* I can't recall any critic I have documented calling *Tom Jones* a *Bildungsroman,* but Tom and Sophia are considerably more experienced by the end of the novel, and at the start of the novel Tom is a foundling baby. But both Raimondi and Mirto Golo Stone call *I promessi sposi* a *Bildungsroman,*[63] and we have yet to see more ways in which that novel and *Tom Jones* are remarkably alike. Both Lucia and Sophia are at times maidens in distress. Lucia's brief and terrifying abduction is straight out of a "Gothic" novel. And in London, before Blifil is exposed and Tom is known to be Squire Allworthy's nephew, Squire Western is still so intent on Sophia's marrying Blifil that he imprisons her in his lodgings until his sister obtains Sophia's release. Both Sophia and Lucia are pretty girls, and pretty girls, even in odysseys, are less likely to undergo as much as men in odysseys. By the end of the novel Sophia is considerably more experienced but probably not as much more experienced as Tom is. But, as I've indicated above, there is a real question as to how much more Lucia has learned and how much more experienced she is at the end of *I promessi sposi.* We have just seen that by the end of that novel Renzo, unlike some other characters in the novel, has learned that truth is not prior to experience but is gained through experience, and that is real *Bildung.* But Fielding asserts that Tom the "fornicator" supposedly becomes prudent at the end of *Tom Jones,* and Renzo, at the end of *I promessi sposi,* also supposedly learns to be more prudent. When we get to discussions of the characters, these developments, supposititious or not, will necessitate a fair amount of commentary.

We have seen in a Miller quotation above that Fielding considered *Tom Jones* to be comic, and indeed through all difficulties and hazards Tom and Sophia come to an idealized happy marriage at the end of the novel. And the general tone of *Tom Jones* is light and playful. Christianity is sometimes

[61]. "Seicento," p. 96.

[62]. "Multiple Structures and the Unity of *Tom Jones,*" *Criticism* 14 (1972): 229.

[63]. See Raimondi, p. 3, and see Stone's "Contro la modernità e la cultura borghese: *I promessi sposi* e l'ascesa del romanzo italiano," *Modern Language Notes* 107 (1992): 124.

considered comic because, after the trials and tribulations of earthly life, orthodox Christians supposedly dwell happily in heaven after their deaths. In this sense the ending of *I promessi sposi* is comic because, like Tom and Sophia, Renzo and Lucia come to an idealized happy marriage. But the greater part of what has preceded that marriage doesn't seem comic at all, the general tone is somber, and the lengthy description of the plague is downright grim and ghastly. Nonetheless, the comic does sometimes find its way into the body of the novel. The comic is most evident in the characterization of don Abbondio. D. M. White, for one, notes how comical don Abbondio is,[64] and he even says that don Abbondio is in Italian literature what Dickens's Mr. Micawber, in *David Copperfield*, is in English literature.[65] Fra Cristoforo was earlier a vigorous man out in the world by the name of Lodovico who had at least once thought of becoming a monk and who, after he kills a man in a fight, has to take refuge in a monastery and become a monk, and for the rest of his life he is purportedly a paragon of saintliness. Don Abbondio doesn't seem very religious at all, but he decided from the outset to become a priest because the priesthood seemed to offer him an easy, untroubled life, and indeed perhaps being confronted by the *bravi* who forbid the marriage is a major crisis in his life. And don Abbondio needs an easy life, for he has anxiety neurosis and so worries about almost everything. A good example of how humorous he is can be seen in the following situation. The marriage being forbidden, Agnese, a resourceful woman, comes up with another way in which Renzo and Lucia can be married. Timid Lucia isn't keen about the plan but agrees to go through with it. And so Renzo gets two witnesses and brings them with Lucia to don Abbondio's house, where Perpetua lets them in. Before don Abbondio

> Renzo mise a proferire le parole: "Signor curato, in presenza di questi testimoni, quest'è mia moglie." . . . La poveretta [Lucia], con quella sua voce soave . . . aveva appena potuto proferire "e questo . . ." que don Abbondio le aveva buttato sgarbatamente il tappeto sulla testa e sul viso, per impedirle di pronunziare intera la formola. (Ch. VIII [p. 104])

> [Renzo began by saying the words: "Reverend father, in the presence of these witnesses, this is my wife." . . . The poor girl [Lucia], in her gentle voice . . . had hardly been able to say "and

---

64. Pp. 147-48.
65. Pp. 130-31.

this . . ." when don Abbondio had rudely thrown the tablecloth over her head and face, in order to prevent her from saying in entirety the formula.]

Then don Abbondio flees to another room, locks himself in, and bellows out the window that there are people in the house. It is not as easy to notice, but Norbert Jonard rightly points out that there are instances of the humor of the little people in the novel,[66] and a likely place to see this is in the bread-riots sequence in Milan. But overall *I promessi sposi* is no hilarious novel. *Tom Jones* is so manifestly comic that there seems to be little need for commentary, but a few remarks are in order. Damrosch rightly says: "While appreciating Western's sheer comic energy one ought not to overlook his meanness and cruelty,"[67] and, "his meanness and cruelty" aside, this coarse, boozy squire who spews out words rather than speaks them is, with the Falstaff of Shakespeare's *I Henry IV* and Dickens's Mr. Micawber, one of the greatest comic creations in English literature. The only other things in *Tom Jones* which are as comic as Squire Western is are the sequence of events at the inn at Upton and the incident in which Mrs. Partridge attacks her husband because she thinks he has been unfaithful. Of the two "interpolated tales" in *Tom Jones* it struck me during this rereading that Fielding might have cut down Mrs. Fitzpatrick's story quite a bit, but at that both she and her estranged husband figure importantly in the plot. Of the other, that of the Man of the Hill, Ian Watt speaks of "a few excrescences [in *Tom Jones*] such as the interpolated story of the Man of the Hill . . . ."[68] Some other critics also seem bothered by the presence of this story in the novel. Indeed, it is not related to the main plot, but I think it is important for two reasons, the last relevant to our concerns here. First, the account of the Man of the Hill's youthful "follies" resonates to some of Tom's earlier "follies" although when Tom leaves him differences appear. But, aside from that, I think the Man of the Hill and his story belong in *Tom Jones* for the following reason. Granted, the Man of the Hill is an old puritan, but he says this:

"Man alone hath basely dishonoured his own Nature, and
by Dishonesty, Cruelty, Ingratitude, and accursed Treachery,
hath called his Maker's Goodness in Question, by puzzling us to

66. "Réflexions sur le comique dans les *Promessi sposi*," *Revue des Études Italiennes* 20 (1974): 138.
67. P. 121.
68. "Fielding as Novelist: *Tom Jones*," in Bloom, p. 15.

account how a benevolent Being should form so imperfect and
so vile an Animal."[69]

Aside from dangerous animals, diseases, extremes of heat and cold, and
natural disasters the world would be a quite wonderful place if it weren't
for what a great many humans have made and still do make of the world.
The Man of the Hill's negative note is just what is needed amidst the comic
cheer and even optimism of *Tom Jones*. Of course in the eighteenth century
it was easier to be cheerful than it has been in the nineteenth and twentieth
centuries. But at that in his *Amelia* a few years later Fielding shows the dark
shades of incipient capitalism.[70]

We have seen that Fielding considered his novels epics in prose. And
indeed, epics in verse are very novelistic. I would not flatly and absolutely
call *Tom Jones* and *I promessi sposi* epics, but I see in both of them epic
qualities. In all verse epics except Milton's too-pedantic *Paradise Lost*
there is vigorous action overall, and in these two novels, with the lovers
separated early and they thereafter sometimes experiencing considerable
difficulties before peaceful marriages at the end of the novels, there is
quite a bit of action and sometimes even "adventure." And most epics
have strong "story" lines, and these two novels, and especially with the
marriage initially forbidden *I promessi sposi*, have strong "story" lines of
epic proportions. Ann Rosalind Jones is helpful here, for she points out
that *I promessi sposi* has an epic sense of "the unity of man and his external
world."[71] And in the earlier *Tom Jones* of course man is still close to nature.
The very literary *Paradise Lost* in the seventeenth century is the most
recent verse epic I know of, and of course there are differences between
early, "naive" epics and modern novels. For further on Jones points out
that *I promessi sposi* does not have the unanalyzed time of the epic and
that Manzoni's conception of time is post-epic.[72] Indeed, in *I promessi sposi*
some passages give a rather exact sense of the passing of time, and in

---

[69.] Citations from Fielding in my text are to *The History of Tom Jones, a Foundling*,
introd. and commentary Martin C. Battestin, text ed. Fredson Bowers, The
Wesleyan Edition of the Works of Henry Fielding (Middletown, Conn.: Wesleyan
U Press, 1975), 2 vols. Here Bk. VIII, Ch. xv (I, 484). A further reference will
be given in the text.

[70.] For an excellent discussion of the two "interpolated tales" see Miller, pp. 258-74
passim.

[71.] "Manzoni's *Promessi sposi* and Lukács' *Theorie des Romans*," *Arcadia* 11 (1976):
127.

[72.] Pp. 135 and 136.

other passages there is a far vaguer sense of time.[73] *Tom Jones* covers Tom's life from infancy through marriage, and in parts of the novel time passes rather vaguely and carelessly, but in the London books often quick and decisive action becomes important, and in them time becomes more of a factor. Of course *Tom Jones* and *I promessi sposi* can't, strictly speaking, be epics, but in the development and drama of their fictions they have marked epic qualities.

We have seen that Manzoni was deeply religious, and at the same time and somewhat contradictorily that in *I promessi sposi* there is a mainly liberal historicist thrust. Manzoni was not a mainstream Catholic but rather was a Jansenist Catholic or was at least heavily influenced by Jansenism.[74] And indeed, Jansenism was or is a liberal, even somewhat subversive variant of Catholicism.[75] And note this: "It may be noted, incidentally, that no Jesuits are mentioned in *I promessi sposi*, though it is set in a period when they were at the height of their power."[76] There is a distinct moral aim in *I promessi sposi*, for better or for worse, and there is also a distinct moral aim in *Tom Jones*, for at its end Fielding wants us to believe that Tom the "fornicator" learns to be prudent. And though he wasn't nearly so religious as Manzoni, Fielding in fact was a religious man. For Martin C. Battestin says: "Fielding's morality and his religion are founded upon the benevolist theories inculcated by the Latitudinarians and given additional currency by Shaftsbury."[77] And Battestin says elsewhere and quite dubiously: "the fortunate contingencies and surprising turns which affect the course of events in *Tom Jones* . . . have an essential function in the expression of Fielding's Christian vision of life."[78] But of course Battestin is an ardent advocate of prudence. At any rate, not just one but both ot these great novels were written by religious liberals.

[73.] On this topic see Gabriel Lanyi, "Plot-Time and Rhythm in Manzoni's *I promessi sposi*," *Modern Language Notes* 83 (1978): 36-51 passim.

[74.] See Colquhoun, pp. 610-11, and "Jansénisme," in *Grand Dictionnaire Encyclopédique Larousse* (Paris: Librairie Larousse, 1984): VI, 5796-97, though the latter is more on the history of Jansenism than on doctrine.

[75.] Colquhoun, p. 610.

[76.] Colquhoun, p. 611.

[77.] "Introduction," in *Twentieth Century Interpretations of* Tom Jones, ed. Battestin, Twentieth Century Interpretations (Englewood Cliffs, NJ: Prentice-Hall, 1968) 9.

[78.] "*Tom Jones*: The Argument of Design," in Bloom, pp. 62-63.

But in both novels the religious or moral aim is subverted. For in his little book *The Panzaic Principle*[79] Wayne Burns points out that quite a number of great literary works, and especially great novels, are Panzaic, i.e., in them the ideals of characters or the author or both are undercut by the numerous realities elsewhere in the work. And there is authorial idealization of characters in both these novels, albeit considerably more in *I promessi sposi*. We have seen, for instance, that Fielding's Squire Allworthy is purportedly all goodness and, for a man of his age, remarkably innocent. Religion is built so deeply into *I promessi sposi* that, aside from some disorderly little people in Milan during the bread riots mainly, all the humble or little people in the novel are "nice," "good" Catholics. Nonetheless, the novel manages to be Panzaic, as is also *Tom Jones*. One major character in *I promessi sposi* is Panzaic, and a minor character, both by virtue of Manzoni's approach to her and by virtue of her one recorded and reprehensible act after she is in the convent, functions Panzaically. Earlier I asserted that, although Manzoni couldn't have acknowledged it, don Rodrigo is his greatest character, and don Rodrigo of course is a Panzaic character. And of course he is also a "villain." He is a powerful man, and he uses force to prevent Lucia's marriage to Renzo, and he has the Innominato abduct her. Fortunately, the Innominato releases her, but if don Rodrigo had ever gotten hold of her, pious Lucia would never have yielded to him, and don Rodrigo would have had to rape her, and as the wealthy Innominato committed his "crimes" with impunity, the powerful and wealthy don Rodrigo could surely commit rape with impunity. And it is not exactly uncommon that Panzaic characters are "villains." The dwarf Quilp in Dickens's *The Old Curiosity Shop* is both Panzaic and a "villain." But to paint don Rodrigo as a totally black "villain" is reductive. There are complications. He is not necessarily an accomplished don Juan and is not always at ease in the role of a don Juan. At times he is concerned about Lucia's welfare and well being. And when Fra Cristoforo confronts him to speak for Renzo and Lucia, don Rodrigo shows that he can be introspective.[80] In the *lazzaretto* don Rodrigo

---

79. (Vancouver, BC: Pendejo Press [n.d.]), see passim. Indeed, in the first part of this book Burns discusses *Tom Jones* (see pp. 8-13), but his discussion is as much or more on Ian Watt's criticism as it is on the novel.

80. See again Ciotti, pp. 70-82 passim, and Pallotta, "Characterization," pp. 43-55 passim, and see especially Pallotta's "Fra Cristoforo and Don Rodrigo: The Words That Wound," *Italica* 67 (1990): 335-52 passim. See also Girardi, "Carattere e destino del personaggio manzoniano: don Rodrigo," *Rivista di studi italiani* 3.2 (1985): 24-36 passim.

Paul Green

is obviously dying from the plague, and Ernst Nef says: "Per quanto poi reguarda Don Rodrigo, Manzoni non si preoccupa di presentarci il modo in cui egli si ammala e muore come una manifestazione della giusta ira del Signore contro un colpevole."[81] ["As regards don Rodrigo, Manzoni does not preoccupy himself to present the manner of his death as a manifestation of the just anger of the Lord against a guilty man."] Still it does look as if Manzoni felt obliged to kill off "wicked" don Rodrigo, but the effects of the plague were devastating. At the time of the plague the population of Milan went down from 250, 000 to 60, 000.[82] So it is not really surprising that don Rodrigo contracts a fatal case of the plague. The other character who functions Panzaically in the novel is Gertrude, the nun of Monza. The character Gertrude was based on an historical personage by the name of Marianna.[83] Convents and monasteries are old and venerated institutions in the Catholic church, but at the same time they are one of the worst features of Catholicism, with women shut away from men and living homoerotically with women and with men shut away from women and living homoerotically with men. And the atmosphere in convents and monasteries has to be psychopathological. Manzoni devotes two chapters to Gertrude before she goes into the convent, in the convent she once becomes part of the main plot, I wish Manzoni had told more about her after she is in the convent, but at that the question has been raised as to why Manzoni developed so minor a character as Gertrude as much as he did.[84] Gertrude is the daughter of an impoverished "nobleman" who wanted all his money to go to his son, so from birth the pretty Gertrude is destined to go into a convent. And when the time comes for her to go into the convent, the poor girl is so browbeaten that she says she is entering the convent voluntarily. Nonetheless, earlier she got involved with one Egidio, and Francesco Maggini asserts that Gertrude was seduced by Egidio.[85] Of course Manzoni doesn't like to see this pretty girl railroaded into a convent, but Manzoni was also rather severe towards youth and considered passion the root cause of "evil." The question arises as to whether he had objections to convents and monasteries, but to my knowledge the Jansenism by which he was heavily influenced makes no objection to the convent-monastery system. It is useful to raise the question, but I cannot answer it. And of

[81]. "Caso e provvidenza nei *Promessi sposi*," *Modern Language Notes* 85 (1970): 18.

[82]. Wall, p. 44.

[83]. Marion Facinger Freidson, "The Meaning of Gertrude in *I promessi sposi*," *Italica* 28 (1951): 28.

[84]. By Freidson, p. 27.

[85]. "Dante e Manzoni," *Rassegna della letteratura italiana* 62 (1958): 198.

course Gertrude didn't want to go into the convent. Before she goes into the convent, Gertrude is to be pitied. But once in the pathological atmosphere of the convent, Gertrude and her case are a different story. For it is Gertrude who persuades Lucia to go out of the convent and onto the country road, and she knows full well that when Lucia goes out, she will be abducted. I have read *I promessi sposi* four times, and i haven't seen it at all, but Marion Facinger Freidson asserts that Gertrude betrays Lucia because of her relationship with Egidio.[86] At any rate, in the convent Gertrude becomes "evil" and so functions Panzaically in this most religious novel.[87] We have seen that Fielding's Squire Allworthy is idealized, and we shall shortly see that there is another case of idealization in *Tom Jones*. And also Fielding wants us to believe that Tom becomes prudent at the end of the novel. And then there are Fielding's introductory chapters, in which he is sometimes the "official" Fielding. So there is need of the Panzaic in *Tom Jones*, and in fact it is present by virtue of Tom's "fornicating" and Western's coarse language. It is not pleasant to be around loud and disorderly people, but disorder in a novel is much easier to take, there is a considerable amount of disorder in *Tom Jones*, and the disorder also functions Panzaically. And *Tom Jones*, because of the "fornicating" or for that and other reasons, has proved upsetting to some readers. Samuel Johnson says: "The loose images in these pieces [including *Tom Jones*] perhaps invite to vice more than the contrast figures alarm us into virtue."[88] And Ford Madox Ford says: "I dislike Tom Jones, the character, because he is a lewd, stupid, and treacherous phenomenon; I dislike Fielding, his chronicler, because he is a bad sort of hypocrite."[89] Well! And Battestin is not the only Fielding critic who is pleased to see that Tom purportedly learns to be prudent at the end of *Tom Jones*.

We have seen that Mazza sees a decided likeness between Sophia and Lucia, and I have pointed out some differences between the two girls, for instance that Sophia is passionate and that Lucia only seems to be properly passionate after she is married. And at that point I said that the

---

86. P. 28.
87. Freidson's article is by far the best article on Gertrude. See passim pp. 27-32. Also, Walter Moretti's "Le 'feste brillanti e faticose' di Gertrude," *Studi e problemi di critica testuale* 2 (1971): 264-72, is helpful on a few points. Gianfranco Grechi's "Gertrude o dell'obbedienza," *Martinella* 23 (1969): 182-85, and Chandler's "Il ritratto di Gertrude," *Giornale storico della letteratura italiana* 141 (1964): 239-42, are both very short and say little that is substantive about Gertrude.
88. From *Gentleman's Magazine* (March 1749), in Rawson, p. 101.
89. From *The English Novel* (1930), in Rawson, p. 342.

main likeness between the girls inheres in their authors' treatment of them, for in fact Fielding and Manzoni idealize Sophia and Lucia. Lucia, as she is presented, is a perfect angel. Renzo is a good Catholic, but Lucia is far more religious than Renzo.[90] Indeed, Lucia is an idealized version of Enrichetta, Manzoni's first wife.[91] And in an amazing coincidence Battestin records that "Sophia Western is in part an idealization of Fielding's first wife, Charlotte Cradock . . . ."[92] That Sophia is idealized can be seen by the flowery language with which she is first introduced. And, again, she is properly passionate, very intelligent and in view of some of the difficulties he gets himself into perhaps more intelligent than Tom, and very pretty. And she is perfect except for a few things: she lies at a time when Tom and Lady Bellaston are also lying, and she hates Blifil, whom it can be inferred she hasn't liked since he freed the caged bird Tom gave her. But there is nothing to like about Blifil, and otherwise Sophia is nice to everyone, even to Molly Seagrim when she must know that Tom was involved with Molly. It could be suggested rather wickedly that if Fielding and Manzoni had allowed Sophia and Lucia to emit stinking flatulence, they would have deidealized their darlings fast, but of course they can't allow that, and indeed the only flatulence in either novel is that of Sophia's coarse father. Lord Fellamar isn't exactly a "nice guy." He tries to have Tom press-ganged at the urging of Lady Bellaston,[93] who is presumably angry at Tom because she has learned he is in love with Sophia. Lord Fellamar is madly in love with Sophia for a time, and that is at a time when Sophia is pretty disillusioned with Tom and when her father hasn't agreed to her marrying Tom, and she could spread her legs for Lord Fellamar, but of course she doesn't. So Lucia is just perfect, and Sophia is nearly perfect, and of course the idealization of both girls is undercut by the Panzaic elements in *Tom Jones* and *I promessi sposi*.

We have seen that Tom and Renzo supposedly learn to be prudent or more prudent at the ends of the novels and also that Renzo is a good Catholic but not as religious as Lucia. We have also seen that, unlike Tom, Renzo is a "good" repressed fellow during his odyssey and separation from Lucia. There are only two situations in which Renzo's behavior is

---

[90.] This fact is noted by Franco Fido in "*I promessi sposi* come sottotesto in alcuni romanzi dell'ottocento," *Italica* 61 (1984): 102.

[91.] Lakebrink, pp. 196-97.

[92.] P. 4.

[93.] This is noted by A. Lentin in "Fielding, Lord Chancellor Hardwicke and the 'Court of Conscience' in *Tom Jones*," *Notes and Queries* 27 (1980): 404.

not model. At the inn in Milan he drinks too much wine and goes to bed drunk. And don Abbondio isn't supposed to tell Renzo why his marriage can't take place, but Renzo gets angry, and don Abbondio has to tell him don Rodrigo is behind it. Then Renzo gets so violently angry he longs to kill don Rodrigo,[94] but don Rodrigo is well protected by his *bravi*, and of course good Christians are supposed to forgive their enemies. It is only when Renzo sees don Rodrigo in the *lazzaretto*, obviously dying from the plague, that Fra Cristoforo can persuade him to forgive don Rodrigo. There is nothing particularly wrong with just once getting very drunk, but when a man gets so violently angry he longs to kill another man, perhaps it is in order for him to learn to be more prudent. Tom's case is another matter altogether. Of course at the end of the novel he is married to his beloved Sophia, whom he, like Fielding, has idealized. And of course Renzo and Tom are characters in novels, and after a few years of marriage they have no more life. But if we assume for our purposes that Tom's life goes on, it seems highly unlikely that he would be all that prudent. He saw Molly Seagrim and fell in love with her, and he might well, albeit he loves Sophia dearly, see someone else and fall in love with her. Or he might encounter a woman, such as Mrs. Waters, with designs on him, and in his good-natured way yield to her. Tom's "prudence" seems to be Fielding's and some critics' wishful thinking. We have gotten here to the novels' endings, and there is a need to say a bit more about the idealized happy endings, with Tom and Sophia and Renzo and Lucia living in perfect bliss and presumably being blessed with children who are all model children. Fielding reports this at the end of *Tom Jones*:

> Mr. *Jones* appears to be the happiest of all human Kind; For what Happiness this World affords equal to the Possession of such a Woman as *Sophia*, I sincerely own I have never yet discovered. (Bk. XVIII, Ch. xiii [II, 979])

And Manzoni reports this at the end of *I promessi sposi*:

> Prima que finisse l'anno del matrimonio, venne alla luce una bella creatura, e, come se fosse fatto apposta per dar subito opportunità a Renzo d'adempire quella sua magnanima promessa, fu una bambina; e potete credere che le fu messo nome Maria . . . . (Ch. XXXVIII [p. 540])

---

94. See on this Raimondi, p. 5.

[Before the end of the first year of marriage, a beautiful baby
was born, and, as if it was done fittingly to give opportunity to
Renzo to fulfill his magnanimous promise, it was a girl; and you
can believe she was named Maria . . . .]

And of course it would be a beautiful baby and would be named Maria
after the supposititious "Virgin." We can accept that at the end of both
novels the couples marry, but more remains to be said. It is unlikely that
Renzo would be unfaithful, but Tom most likely would be unfaithful, and
that could cause fierce disputes. And when couples are courting or even
engaged, they take special care to show themselves to each other at their
best. When they marry, they relax, and sometimes husbands and wives see
each other at their worst. and in marriages usually more things come up to
quarrel about than during the courting period. The perfect bliss of these
two marriages is pure poppycock, and these endings are undercut by the
Panzaic elements in both novels.

We have seen that Renzo and Lucia are faithful Catholics and that Lucia
is so pious she hardly dares commit the slightest "sin." And Tom is a Christian
who frequently "sins" and who always repents for his "sins." Butler rightly
says that Tom is just fooling himself when he repents.[95] Tom suffers most
and longest from guilt feelings—in fact until he learns that his mother is
actually Bridget, Squire Allworthy's sister—after Partridge sees Mrs. Waters
in London and tells Tom she is Jenny Jones, his purported mother. And if
Tom had gone to bed with his mother, there would be nothing wrong in
it. If there is mutual consent and no force or rape, incest is alright, but if
a child is born from an incestuous relationship whose mother, say, is also
his or her grandmother, there is a kind of mess. To my knowledge, not
a word is said in *Tom Jones* about Sophia vis-à-vis religion. Sophia dearly
loves her coarse, boozy father, who probably never goes to church and
has little or no interest in religion. But she has another parental role
model in her politic, far more "civilized" aunt, and as Sophia is a demure,
well-behaved, even almost "decorous" girl, she must take her aunt as a role
model far more than the father she is so unlike. Sophia is of course quite
intelligent, but in the pre-Darwinian, pre-Freudian eighteenth century it
was considerably easier and more common to be sincerely religious than
it is now. And Sophia marries Tom, who is a Christian. I have no evidence
one way or the other, but as Sophia is a carefully "good" girl, I infer that
she accepts the doctrines of the Church of England. At any rate, three of
the four protagonists in these two novels are definitely religious.

[95.] *Unruly*, p. 106.

We have seen that Renzo is arrested in the morning at the inn in Milan, escapes with the help of the crowd, flees to Bergamo, and after a time has to move to another locality and live under an assumed name. And he was not arrested for rioting. Why then was he arrested? At that time in Italy when one stayed at an inn, it was illegal to refuse to give one's name to the innkeeper. Renzo, in his drunkenness, does tell his name to a person or two in the inn, but he has just had to flee from his native village, I infer he may have feared that don Rodrigo had some of his men looking for him, and, for that or another reason, he refuses to give his name to the innkeeper, but in the morning his name is known, probably from others at the inn to whom he has told his name. By the time he marries Lucia, he has been granted a dispensation which frees him from any further legal trouble. Tom also is arrested, there is no sympathetic crowd present to free him, and so he has to spend a considerable amount of time in jail. Why is he arrested? Fitzpatrick turns up in London and is still convinced that Tom has been involved with his estranged wife, and when he encounters Tom, Fitzpatrick forces him into a fight in which Tom seriously wounds him, and so Tom is put in jail. Later, after Fitzpatrick has recovered some, he acknowledges that he, not Tom, started the fight, and so Tom is released. And then his fortunes suddenly and in cases almost miraculously get amazingly better. Tom doesn't want to fight and is forced to fight, and when he is released from jail, he is exonerated. Renzo is being very wary in Milan and is arrested because of a technicality, his "crime" does no harm to anyone, and his dispensation at the end of the novel frees him from further prosecution. Technically, Renzo breaks the law, but in essence he does nothing wrong by refusing to give his name to the innkeeper.

It is rather amazing how like these two novels are, especially as there is no clear evidence that Manzoni had ever read *Tom Jones*, but of course there are a number of differences between them, and to these we must now come. We have seen that Fielding, being opposed to Richardson in everything, deliberately limits himself in the writing of *Tom Jones*. Richardson is the father of the psychological novel, and so Fielding excludes the psychological from *Tom Jones*, and so *Tom Jones* is a novel with a lot of action in it. But of course Fielding has to supply motivation for actions, and the motivation in *Tom Jones* is always very good and carefully explained. But does the lack of psychology in *Tom Jones* harm the novel? When Ian Watt writes on *Tom Jones*, he is often concerned with the deliberate limitations on the novel, and he says:

> Fielding's avoidance of the subjective dimension [in *Tom Jones*] . . . is quite intentional: but that does not, of course, mean that it has no drawbacks, for it undoubtedly has, and they

become very apparent whenever important emotional climaxes are reached.[96]

In my latest rereading of *Tom Jones*, I didn't notice this lack in emotional climaxes, and I think Watt is flatly wrong. There are some great psychological novels, Richardson's *Clarissa* for one, but all novels need not be psychological novels. We have seen that there is more idealization of characters in *I promessi sposi* than in *Tom Jones*. I know nothing about the historical Borromeo, but as Manzoni presents him, he is just perfect. And Fra Cristoforo, after he becomes a monk, is just saintly—except that in times of stress traces of the old and even violent Lodovico come back. But of course all the characters in *I promessi sposi* are not idealized, and in depicting some of the other characters Manzoni often shows considerable psychological acuity. Giovanni Ghetti Abruzzi speaks of "il realismo storico e psicologico del dialogo"[97] ["the historical and psychological realism of the dialogue"] in *I promessi sposi*, and he particularly points out the psychological elements in the *lazzaretto* sequence.[98] Thus we have the first difference: Manzoni is psychological, and Fielding is not.

The second difference we can pass over quickly. We have seen that Fielding and Manzoni were in the main religious liberals. In his youth Manzoni was deeply influenced by things French and was an unbeliever, but by the time he had started *Fermo e Lucia* [*Fermo and Lucia*], the first version of *I promessi sposi*, he had become a mainly Jansenist Catholic. And, as we have seen, religion is built deep into *I promessi sposi*, but the religion is undercut. Religion comes up a number of times in *Tom Jones*, but it is not really a religious novel at all, and Fielding obviously doesn't like Thwackum's fundamentalism before the era of fundamentalism. And though I am hardly steeped in Fielding biography, I infer that Fielding wasn't terribly religious although in his "official" self there is a certain amount of Christian moralism. Thus the second difference: Manzoni was deeply religious, and Fielding seems to have been a mainly nominal believer.

We have already seen that *I promessi sposi* is an historical novel written in the early nineteenth century, and *Tom Jones* of course is a contemporary eighteenth-century novel. *Tom Jones* was published in 1749, it is a very long novel that Fielding must have worked on for quite some time, and the events in *Tom Jones* can be dated as taking place in 1745, which must

---

96. P. 273.
97. "Un dialogo d'amore nei *Promessi sposi*," *Parola del popolo* 66 (1974): 62.
98. P. 61.

be the year Fielding began work on the novel. How do we know? Again, it can be determined because there is a minor political dimension in *Tom Jones*, frequent references to the Jacobite rebellion. The references to the rebellion in *Tom Jones* are all sketchy, Manzoni as an historical novelist was of course influenced by Sir Walter Scott and had read Scott's *Waverley*, and *Waverley* provides a gloss on *Tom Jones*, for there is considerably more on the Jacobite rebellion in *Waverley*. From *Waverley* we learn that the rebellion had great strength in Scotland, and especially in the Scottish Highlands. The fullest commentary I've found on this aspect of *Tom Jones* is Thomas R. Cleary's "Jacobitism in *Tom Jones*: The Basis for an Hypothesis."[99] Fielding was anti-Jacobite.[100]

Fielding wants Tom to be prudent at the end of *Tom Jones*, he doesn't exactly approve of Tom's "fornicating" but considers other "sins" to be far worse, and for him "fornicating" is just a venial "sin," but in fact at least at Upton he describes the "fornicating" with great gusto. And the "fornicating" makes *Tom Jones* an erotic novel. Manzoni's don Rodrigo longs to "fornicate" with Lucia, and Manzoni must punish him for his "sins" by death from the plague although of course an incredibly large number of people did die from the plague. The "pure" Lucia can only be passionate after her marriage, when she has numerous babies. During his prolonged odyssey and separation from Lucia Renzo of course doesn't "fornicate." In Bergamo and the other locality in which he lives some girls should have gotten interested in him and perhaps a few might even have tried to seduce him, but of course Manzoni says not a word about any girls during Renzo's odyssey. So *I promessi sposi* is not an erotic novel, or at most it is marginally erotic by virtue of don Rodrigo's longing to "fornicate."

As we have seen, Manzoni's deep religiosity gives him a pessimistic view of the human condition and humanity which is somewhat at odds with his progressive historicism. *I promessi sposi* at least ends happily for Renzo and Lucia if not for Italy, there are touches of the comic in the novel, but otherwise and overall *I promessi sposi* is a serious, even somber novel. And as we have also seen, in *Tom Jones*, through all dangers and difficulties, the tone is mainly cheerful, and it is a comic, optimistic novel. And that is the reason I think it is important to have in the novel the Man of the Hill's dark view of humanity. Generally in the preindustrial eighteenth century it was considerably easier to be cheerful than it has been in the nineteenth and twentieth centuries for anyone as sensitive and introspective as Manzoni was.

---

99. *Philological Quarterly* 52 (1973): 239-51 passim.
100. Cleary, p. 241.

The next difference has also come up before. Manzoni revolutionarily chose for his protagonists two "rednecks." Manzoni was writing in the "romantic" era. He disliked "romantic" extravagances, medievalism, etc., but he thought he was "romantic" in one sense, for, following Schlegel and Mme de Staël, he held that "romanticism" is Christian[101] when in fact "romanticism" is rebellious albeit too often idealistic. But Manzoni's siding with the little people is very "romantic," for, for example, the English "romantic" poet William Wordsworth was also very concerned about humble and "lowly" people. However, at the end of *I promessi sposi*, Renzo, albeit he still can't read very well, has become entrepreneurial and even invested money with his cousin Bortolo and so become petty bourgeois. And of course Sophia is the daughter of a squire and so "gentry." Tom initially is a bastard and foundling, but he is raised as a son by Squire Allworthy, and at the end of *Tom Jones* Tom is learned to be the bastard nephew of Squire Allworthy and becomes his heir and so becomes "gentry."

Tom Jones, aside from Fielding's introductory chapters and its minor political dimension on Jacobitism, is all or simply the story of Tom and Sophia and their relations and acquaintances. And *I promessi sposi* is a richer novel, a novel with more dimensions. Manzoni has a great fiction or story about the forbidden marriage of Renzo and Lucia and their ensuing troubles, *I promessi sposi* is a very long novel, I have no statistics available, but at least one third of *I promessi sposi* is concerned with other characters and events and not with Renzo and Lucia. Near the end of the novel don Rodrigo is obviously dying from the plague, Fra Cristoforo catches the plague while helping in the *lazzaretto* and dies of it, and both are major characters in the novel. And Lucia falls ill from the plague but fortunately recovers. Manzoni has a great fiction, the lengthy and ghastly description of the plague concerns far more people and devastation than just three characters and the fiction proper, and the description of the plague is the greatest thing in the novel. Consider this:

> La peste que il tribunale della sanita aveva temuto che potesse entrar con le bande alemanno nel milanese, c'era entrata davvero, come è noto, ed è noto parimente che non si fermò qui, ma invase e spopulo una buona parte d'Italia. (Ch. XXXI [p. 423])

> [The plague that the tribunal of public health had feared would enter with the German soldiers into Milan had in fact come,

---

101. Peer, p. 267.

as has been noted, and it has been noted likewise that it didn't
stop there, but invaded elsewhere and decimated a considerable
part of the population of Italy.]

And consider this later statement: "la furia del contagio andò sempre
crescendo" (Ch. XXXII [p. 445]) ["the fury of the contagion continued,
always growing"].

Finally, we have seen that the only thing really erotic in *I promessi sposi*
is don Rodrigo's longing to "fornicate," Renzo and Lucia love each other
dearly and steadfastly, but at the start of the novel they are engaged and
expect to be married in a day or two, and so *I promessi sposi* is far more a
novel about marriage, unerotic as it is, than about love. In *Tom Jones* Tom
is first in love with the "lowly" Molly Seagrim, but it is not long before he
is madly in love with Sophia. And Sophia comes to love Tom early in the
novel even though she always holds that she will never marry without her
father's consent, and as Tom is believed to be a bastard of "lowly" birth,
she must think she can never marry him. And of course it is only at the
end of the novel, when Tom is still a bastard but now bastard "gentry,"
that her father consents to and even urges her to marry Tom, and then
she is very disillusioned with Tom because she knows that for a time he
was Lady Bellaston's kept man and has to consider whether she can accept
him, but in a remarkably short time she agrees to marry him. So *Tom Jones*
is a novel about love and not really one about marriage. And as Tom is a
bastard and long considered one of "lowly" birth, he doesn't have all the
privileges legitimately born, well to do people have. And so *Tom Jones* is
also a novel about birth.

I've had to work long on this essay, this essay has gotten almost too
long, and still I could go on discussing numerous issues and critical
comments—pro and con—on these two novels. And it has been especially
pleasurable to work on this, my first eighteenth-century essay, my third
written foray into Italian literature, and my first Italian essay. And the
greatest pleasure in the project has been to work on *I promessi sposi* and
things Italian. Again, *I promessi sposi* and Stendhal's *La Chartreuse de Parme*
have rightly been called the greatest novels on Italy. Manzoni published
quite a number of poems, Luigi Tonelli denies that *I promessi sposi* is a
poetic novel,[102] but I disagree with Tonelli and am sure some Manzoni
critics would also disagree, and the poetry in the novel gives it an added
dimension. From *I promessi sposi* and probably other sources we know that
the Italian people have suffered a lot, and still there are many miseries

---

[102] *La critica letteraria italiana* (Bari: Gius, Laterza e Figli, 1914) 218.

in Italy, especially in the mainly poor agricultural South of Italy. In recent decades France has been in decline, but earlier it was a country of remarkable achievements, and, generally speaking, the French are far more alive than we in an Anglo-Saxon culture are. And spoken French is very elegant. But somehow there is no magic about the French and things French. The Italians, generally speaking, are also far more alive than we in an Anglo-Saxon culture are. Of the languages I know Swedish is the most beautiful and elegant, and Italian is the second most beautiful. And there is a kind of magic about the language and numerous things Italian, despite the many miseries of Italy.[103]

[103.] All translations from the Italian in this essay, except for standardly translated titles, are mine.

IV

CLAUSTRATION AND OPENNESS: BRADLEY
HEADSTONE AND "FRIENDS"

M uch has been written about *Our Mutual Friend*, and of that output a preponderance focuses implicitly or explicitly—and with considerable justification—on the money-excrement theme and its entailments.[1] What I am concerned with here involves some entailments even as it turns our attention in other directions. But respectability and money have a dysfunctionally symbiotic relationship, and respectability is the guiding ideal for the Bradley Headstone we first meet. The direct issue of possession and acquisition enters into his story only peripherally,

---

[1] See, for example, J. Hillis Miller, *Charles Dickens: The World of His Novels* (Cambridge, Mass.: Harvard U Press, 1958) 294-95; Michael Steig, "Dickens' Excremental Vision," *Victorian Studies* 13 (1970): 339; Kenneth Muir, "Image and Structure in *Our Mutual Friend*," *Essays and Studies* NS 19 (1966): 96-97 (there was of course excrement in the dust mounds, Muir points out [p. 97] that "The river was in fact the main sewer of London," and there is plenty of moneygrubbing in the novel's river plot); Earle Davis, *The Flint and the Flame: The Artistry of Charles Dickens* (Columbia: U of Missouri Press, 1963) 265-66; Edgar Johnson, *Charles Dickens: His Tragedy and Triumph* (New York: Simon and Schuster, 1952) II, 1026-31; and Nancy Aycock Metz, "The Artistic Reclamation of Waste in *Our Mutual Friend*," *Nineteenth Century Fiction* 34 (1979): 69-70, and note especially her statement (p. 69) that "Since Humphry House first made explicit the connection between the Harmon dustheaps and the contents of Victorian privies, nearly every critic of the novel has had something to say about the way this symbol works."

as the brutal irony concomitant on his abortive breakthrough to passion and the entanglements that breakthrough leads to. But note that Cathy Shuman says this about Bradley's teaching and mentality: "Bradley's 'wholesale warehouse' of a brain is firmly associated with the market economy so savagely critiqued throughout the novel."[2] Bradley handles his attempt to find love badly enough (though to say that much need not suggest passion should be *managed*), this particular passion is doomed to frustration, and—most important of all—Bradley is so limited and so warped by his personal development that the breakthrough to passion is fraught with danger in any case. Equipped with only a slow-working, plodding mind, Bradley has had to repress himself excessively in order to master his teaching subject matter, and of course he is not an aware man and so has accepted society's values in toto.

Dickens allows us no illusion that Bradley is an admirable figure even at the start. His satire of Bradley, harsh and direct at first, points up Bradley's inadequacy in the little world of the schoolroom even before he has really ventured into the larger world. But Sylvia Bank Manning rightly says this: "although he [Bradley] never loses his self-righteous obtuseness, he does grow in the course of the novel into something more than . . . [a] satiric cipher . . . . He suffers too much for . . . simple satiric contempt . . . ."[3] But most to the point here is the degree to which Bradley functions—even has a "decent" situation—in that little world. Through hard work he has mastered his subject matter, albeit mechanically, and risen above his obscure origins. Miss Peecher, the girls' teacher, dotes on him and would marry him if he were so inclined. And Miss Peecher is of course educated and "respectable," as Lizzie Hexam is not, and from what Rogue Riderhood says she is not bad looking at all. In his little world Bradley is in a position to command, to control the course events take. In short, he is in some ways in an enviable situation. To say that, however, cannot negate the fact that his feelings do take a course at odds with his situation. Nor is it to deny that respectability, security, and a limited amount of power are finally hollow consolations. Additionally, of course, the larger world outside the schoolroom impinges upon the security and imposed order of that smaller world. In short, I am merely making a case to show that, initially, Bradley could have been far worse off and that, *tactically*, Bradley errs in yielding to his feelings insofar as he ventures out of his smaller world and in the end brings the threatening, chaotic outer world into his classroom in the

---

[2.] "Invigilating *Our Mutual Friend*: Gender and the Legitimation of Professional Authority," *Novel* 28 (1995): 164.

[3.] *Dickens as Satirist* (New Haven, Conn.: Yale U Press, 1971) 211.

person of Rogue Riderhood. And the consequences of Rogue's visit to the schoolroom we know.[4]

The point, of course, is that a Bradley Headstone is obliged to stay, as far as life will allow it, in his carefully circumscribed little world. For such a person or character personal limitations become, sadly, wise prescriptions. Openness, that desideratum for a life which is fully lived, is too much to expect from a Bradley Headstone. We see only too well how Bradley flounders in his attempt to be more open. This occurs of course when he expresses his love to Lizzie, and for the rest of his life he is obliged to close up again. Bradley, of course, is paranoid. This is implicit in what Dickens says of him early on, and it has been stated explicitly by critics.[5] Furthermore, we can safely assert that he is a paranoid schizophrenic. But what does saying that much mean, and why is the issue of openness and claustration so crucial? One major problem for the schizophrenic is the establishing of adequate parameters, which is not the same thing as circumscribing one's actions or way of life but rather its cause. Persons or characters more fortunate do not have such problems with ego integration.[6] They have a far clearer sense of what they are and are not. For them the problem of parameters—though it may arise from time to time—is not something about which to launch a major defensive action. In this way paranoia becomes subsidiary, an *effect* or response to what cannot be handled. Openness is the central issue, even as it penetrates despite all safeguards into closed little classroom worlds.

For Bradley, of course, the main difficulty is not coping with the need for openness as that need arises in the classroom world but rather coping with the need for dealing with troublingly open situations, situations he cannot perforce control, in his hazardous venture into the larger world in quest

---

[4.] The publication of Joel Brattin's "Dickens' Creation of Bradley Headstone" in *Dickens Studies Annual* 14 (1985): 147-65, in no way renders my efforts herein duplicative as Brattin's primary concern is the manuscript of the novel and Dickens's revisions in it vis-à-vis Bradley. Brattin does make a number of good points, for instance in noting (p. 152) "the deceit and the attempted self-deceit of Bradley."

[5.] See Manning, again p. 211, and Philip Hobsbaum, *A Reader's Guide to Charles Dickens* (New York: Farrar, 1972) 263.

[6.] See Géza Róheim, *Magic and Schizophrenia*, ed. Warner Muensterberger and S. H. Posinsky (Bloomington: Midland-Indiana U Press, 1962) 99-102, and especially p. 101. See also-Leonard Manheim, "Dickens' Fools and Madmen," *Dickens Studies Annual* 2 (1972): 82, and especially this statement: "The personality of the schizophrenic is often disintegrated from the very outset . . . ."

of Lizzie. Paranoids cannot deal with the threats they face or the seeming threats that trouble them with or without a verifiable basis. Schizophrenics of whatever sort have difficulties just getting on. But there is a more basic matter here intimately related to openness and self-containment yet despite the intimacy of connection ultimately distinct. I refer to what Freud calls the primary and secondary processes. In *An Outline of Psychoanalysis* he explains these processes thus:

> We assume, as the other natural sciences have taught us to to expect, that in mental life some kind of energy is at work . . . . We seem to recognize that nervous or psychical energy exists in two forms, one freely mobile and the other, by contrast, bound; we speak of cathexes and hypercathexes of the material of the mind and even venture to suppose that a hypercathexis brings about a sort of synthesis of different processes—a synthesis in the course of which free energy is transformed into bound energy. Further than this we have been unable to go . . . .
>
> But behind all . . . uncertainties there lies one new fact . . . . We have learned that processes in the unconscious or in the id obey different laws from those in the preconscious ego. We name these laws in their totality the *primary process*, in contrast to the *secondary process* which regulates events in the preconscious or ego . . . . [7]

This statement more or less clearly gives us the main distinction, but we should note also Anton Ehrenzweig's statement that "the concept of the primary process as the archaic, wholly irrational function of the deep unconscious . . . is now undergoing drastic revision."[8] That he says this to other purposes than mine here should be observed, but what matters more is this further statement: "It has been known all along that the primary process was wholly undifferentiated."[9] The crucial concept here is undifferentiation or mobility as opposed to rigidly structured control. In terms of Freud's statement above, Bradley develops a hypercathexis the object of which is Lizzie. In the process he is obliged to try to break out of the rigid structures of his previous life and way of thinking and to deal with undifferentiated states which in view of Ehrenzweig's thesis have

7. Authorized trans. by James Strachey (New York: Norton, 1949) 44-45.
8. *The Hidden Order of Art: A Study in the Psychology of Artistic Imagination* (Berkeley: U of California Press, 1971) 260.
9. P. 262.

an ordering principle but which to Bradley can only seem frightening and chaotic. The root problem for him is then his inability to deal with whatever is not arbitrarily structured. Openness is antagonistic to set orderings, and in facing situations more frighteningly open than those he has encountered before, Bradley becomes, if indeed he was not before, manifestly mindbound—and with the main concern of *Our Mutual Friend* in view—mentally constipated.[10] In truth, he faces some harrassingly mobile energy in his students, recordedly some time after he has been thrust into the open, but this is again in the smaller world where he can still impose a fairly efficacious (in his view) order and rigidity.[11] Dickens initially mocks Bradley's inability to practice mediation among disciplines as a teacher. And of course he has no conception that mathematics is anal, literature autoerotic, etc. Faced with the task of trying to effect mediations with other people outside the classroom, Bradley can only rage, suffer, assault, kill, and die.[12] Nor is this lamentable fate altogether innately determined. Lacking gifted mental faculties and forcing himself to become an adequate pedant, Bradley has over a period of time destroyed whatever potential there had been in him to live in an open way. Even though Bradley manages to keep

---

10. Speaking of the Veneering group, Davis says (pp. 273-74): "The conversation gives the effect of continual straining over a vacuum of intellectual constipation." In "Homophobia, Misogyny and Capital: The Example of *Our Mutual Friend*," in *Charles Dickens*, ed. Harold Bloom, Modern Critical Views (New York: Chelsea House Publishers, 1987) 252. Eve Kosofsky Sedgwick says: "Sphincter domination is Bradley Headstone's only mode of grappling for the power that is continually flowing away from him. Unfortunately for him, sphincter control can't give him any leverage at all with women–with Lizzie, who simply never engages with him, who eludes him from the start."

11. "Tied up all day with his disciplined show upon him, subdued to the performance of his routine of educational tricks, encircled by a gabbling crowd, he broke loose at night like an ill-tamed wild animal." Citations from Dickens herein are to *Our Mutual Friend* (New York: Bantam, 1990). The Oxford edition of this novel was unavailable to me. Here III, xi (pp. 532-33). A further quotation will be cited in the text.

12. "The 'settled trouble' in Headstone's face is the emotional repression he suffers because of his monomaniacal and acquisitive view of learning and the resultant imbalance in his ability to cope with reality. His book knowledge affords him no wisdom, no comfort, no healing mediation between his mind and the world." So says Kenneth M. Sroka in "Dickens' Metafiction: Readers and Writers in *Oliver Twist, David Copperfield*, and *Our Mutual Friend*," *Dickens Studies Annual* 22 (1993): 53.

functioning till the time of his death, it is no exaggeration to call him mentally ill, and accordingly Ehrenzweig has the last word:

> in mental illness undifferentiated material rises from the unconscious merely to disrupt the more narrowly focused modes of conscious discursive thinking; and the chaos and destruction which we are wont to associate with undifferentiated primary process phantasy overwhelm the patient's reason.[13]

Assaulted from without by rejection, guile, goading, hostility, and blackmail, Bradley is also assaulted from within by an upsurge in his psyche that he cannot control.

In consequence, other things become manifest. Narcissism depends on the *structures* created in accordance with ego ideals. To a Bradley assaults on his self-esteem produce an annihilating descent into undifferentiation and humiliation. This is what happens when Eugene Wrayburn goads him and treats him as a creature of no worth, and in a more experientially prepared way it is what happens when Rogue takes over in Bradley's classroom. Bradley has an ideal of respectability, and if Eugene hasn't made enough assaults on that ideal to shatter it, from the time Rogue, who is in the lowly class Bradley began life in, appears in his classroom and Bradley erases his name from the blackboard, he is plunged fully back into the lowly class he has tried so hard to escape from, and all pretensions to respectability are lost. Thus the ideal is undercut, and the novel is Panzaic.[14] And given his problems, it becomes pointless and tautological to talk about Bradley's selfishness.[15] How could a man that walled in by cautionary inhibitions and that lacking in insight be anything else? Richard T. Gaughan says aptly:

> Headstone embodies the conflict that pervades the novel between what is real and what is accepted as real. His passion for Lizzie alienates him from the conventionalized social world and forces

---

[13.] P. 4.

[14.] See Wayne Burns's *The Panzaic Principle* (Vancouver, BC: Pendejo Press, n.d.) passim. Also, the struggle between Bradley and Rogue into the river and to their deaths undercuts the wealthy and serene harmony of John Harmon and Bella's ideal marriage. And the idealizations of Lizzie, Riah, and possibly also the Boffins are undercut by the many realities in the novel.

[15.] As does Ross H. Dabney, in *Love and Property in the Novels of Dickens* (Berkeley: U of California Press, 1967) 170-71.

him to find a new relationship to himself and his world that can better accommodate that part of him that cannot be reduced to respectability. For this reason, Headstone is a genuinely tragic character. He is forced to confront, on an isolated and intensely personal level, a conflict of values which is characteristic of the world in which he lives.

The tragedy of Bradley Headstone is so powerful that it threatens to dominate the novel and overshadow Harmon's redemptive mission.[16]

But as Bradley is a very limited man, I suspect that he has no idea how representative he is. Juliet McMaster, after quoting the passage in which the class reads Bradley's name from the blackboard, says: "The learned schoolmaster [Bradley], who through his hard-earned literacy has struggled to his present respectable status from a state like Riderhood's, at last finds that literacy is the petard that hoists him."[17] And, lastly, Pam Morris makes a fine point as she says: "Headstone's rejection of shameful origins is represented as a loss also of the class vitality they produce."[18] It is hardly surprising that Bradley, the defensive paranoid, becomes the most memorable of the predatory river rats in *Our Mutual Friend*. He anticipates attacks, he is verifiably attacked at points, and one can scarcely not expect him to become an attacker. Teachers as a class are unusually well behaved, and it was a stroke of inspiration for Dickens to have schoolmaster Bradley commit a brutal assault and a murder. But Bradley of course suffers immeasurably, much as his more gifted creator Dickens was suffering at that stage of his life.[19]

---

16. "Prospecting for Meaning in *Our Mutual Friend*," *Dickens Studies Annual* 19 (1990): 236-37.

17. "Dickens and David Copperfield on the Act of Reading," *English Studies in Canada* 15 (1989): 291.

18. *Dickens's Class Consciousness: A Marginal View* (New York: St. Martin's, 1991) 133. Note this parallel statement by McMaster in *Dickens the Designer* (Totowa, NJ: Barnes and Noble, 1987) 205: "Bradley Headstone is ... [a] character who is presented as partly dead, though in his case no numbness is involved."

19. See Jack Lindsay, *Charles Dickens: A Biographical and Critical Study* (New York: Philosophical Library, 1950) 384. Also, Ray J. Sherer says of Dickens in "Laughter in *Our Mutual Friend*," *Texas Studies in Literature and Language* 13 (1971): 520: "It is well known that ... around the time of his writing of *Our Mutual Friend* ... he had become obsessed with acting out the murder scene from *Oliver Twist* before popular audiences."

Paul Green

Lizzie Hexam is the "friend" to whom it is most instructive to contrast Bradley. Of course, Lizzie makes it very clear that she wants nothing to do with Bradley, but in the ambiguity-charged sequence of events which follow Bradley's initial sortie into the larger world outside the classroom she becomes perforce a "friend" just as Eugene and Rogue do. This is manifest in Eugene and Mortimer Lightwood's careful efforts to prevent Bradley from being prosecuted. Linked to Bradley in spite of her efforts not to be, Lizzie perceives in a way which nourishes openness and undifferentiation. We see in this novel the same kind of juxtaposition there is in *Hard Times*. Bradley is a Gradgrindian drudge,[20] and Lizzie, spared such pedagogic deformation, nourishes her imagination. We know, of course, that imagination was a "romantic" catchword, that insight into the here and now is preferable by far to imagination as fantasy, and that allusions to imagination or feeling were among the maximal suggestions of bodily awareness for a "mid-Victorian" author such as Dickens to work with. But all that being said, we can still recognize the importance of a variation on a theme from *Hard Times*. Lizzie has had a lot of significant experience for one so young, and she has learned to trust her intuitive, exploratory powers.[21] Lizzie is overall hardly an adequate character, but to the extent we can believe in her she has an advantage over the belabored, restricted schoolmaster who comes to want her.

To be sure, Lizzie does flee from London and live in seclusion in the country. But her uneasiness about Bradley is undeniably right, she seems to be a girl with an ideal of a nice marriage, and her relationship with Eugene is fraught with ambiguities he can neither hide from her nor she fail to see. She is serious, capable, too dignified for a waterfront girl,[22] not as sharp as Jenny Wren, pretty, and—unlike some of Dickens's heroines—mature.[23] Her appeal is essentially reflected in her relationship with Charley; it is an Oedipal, sisterly appeal. And as Margaret Flanders Darby says: "She [Lizzie] comes honestly and realistically by her skill on water."[24] So much for what

---

20. However, the Gradgrindian mentality is most directly parodied in Miss Peecher's catechisms of Mary Anne.
21. Note that Bradley explicitly expresses his distrust of imagination to Charley Hexam.
22. Muir says of Lizzie (p. 98): "Quite unrealistically, even when talking with Jenny Wren, she apparently speaks the Queen's English . . . ."
23. Grahame Smith, in *Dickens, Money, and Society* (Berkeley: U of California Press, 1968) 187, says of Lizzie: "she is . . . far removed from the puerilities of many of Dickens' heroines."
24. "Four Women in *Our Mutual Friend*," *Dickensian* 83 (1987): 29. In an extended discussion of Lizzie, Darby fails to say one negative thing about her.

80

can be said positively about Lizzie; otherwise she is a totally inadequate character.[25] The passions of Bradley and Eugene for her require much compliance on the part of readers with Dickens's fiction. The costermongers of Dickens's time escaped "Victorian" prudery, and surely the waterfront characters of his time would have escaped it too. A pretty girl living on the waterfront would have been much pawed and fondled and possibly even raped, and Lizzie supposedly comes to her marriage with Eugene utterly virginal! Lizzie, a post-Ellen Ternan creation, is a throwback to Dickens's Florences, Agneses, and Esthers. And in *Our Mutual Friend* Bella Wilfer is a good creation and even incestuous with her father until she becomes an idealized wife, and her sister Lavinia is a spirited girl who refuses to take any excrement from anybody. To the minimal extent that Lizzie is satisfactory, and in line with our concerns here, she is a good suggestion of openness. But Michael Slater has the last word on Lizzie:

> The mere mention of Jane Eyre and the recollection of her passionate outbursts, her cool wit and her determination to survive, "to keep in good health and not die", exposes Lizzie as the idealized character that she is, fatally lacking in any sort of emotional or intellectual complexity.[26]

The cases of Eugene Wrayburn and Rogue Riderhood are more complicated.[27] Both men are eminently real characters, and both can be open to a degree that Bradley cannot. Yet to go further on the matter requires the making of qualifications with regard to their openness. Eugene has had enough of "gentility" and high society. We see how ruthlessly Dickens treats the Veneering circle and how he presents Eugene, uncomfortable and somewhat dismayed, in the midst of it. Eugene discovers both Lizzie and Bradley by chance, or, more accurately, he discovers Lizzie and in consequence inherits Bradley. And Eugene is open enough to take

---

25. Note, for example, what Peter Lewis says in "The Waste Land of *Our Mutual Friend*," *Durham University Journal* NS 39 (1977): 16: "It is Pleasant [Riderhood], not Lizzie, who is conceived 'realistically'. Lizzie is a much more romanticized and idealized figure, essentially a symbolic character . . . ." For a contrasting view see Smith, again p. 187.

26. *Dickens and Women* (London: J. M. Dent, 1983) 285-86.

27. Charley Hexam, of course, is a quintessentially closed-off character. I do not discuss him at any length because he is far less interesting than Bradley, Eugene, and Rogue. But notice that his shunting off of given people and areas of experience does not arise from *total desperation* as it does for Bradley.

advantage of these acquaintances and do some "slumming." For Lizzie is far "beneath" him, and Bradley's hold on "respectability" is exceedingly tenuous. To be sure, in his law practice Eugene encounters unsavory persons such as Rogue, or persons who simply have a low social standing, but in the cases of Lizzie and Bradley Eugene chooses to mix with them on an off-hours, non-professional basis. This is indeed open and exploratory—to a degree. For with Lizzie he makes no commitments, being unsure what it is he wants from her and perforce being obliged to be somewhat devious. With Bradley he is open insofar as he chooses to enter into a relationship, but we cannot help noticing how much condescension, guile, trickery, and insolence there is in his treatment of Bradley.[28] Perhaps the only time he is even decent to Bradley is when he observes that Bradley is rather too passionate to be a good schoolmaster. Perhaps Bradley does not altogether invite gracious treatment, but Eugene, in his treatment of Bradley, invites the brutal assault he gets. Darby says: "Dickens has worked himself into a corner by the time Eugene catches up with Lizzie on the riverbank,"[29] but it is not Dickens who has worked himself into a corner but rather Eugene, who is thinking just before Bradley assaults him that it is impossible either to leave Lizzie or to marry her. But Lizzie rescues him from the water, and his sickbed decision to marry Lizzie is indeed open, yet, given the circumstances, he can scarcely not marry her and, in so doing, defy "high" society. Audrey Jaffe says:

[28.] Taylor Stoehr, in *Dickens: The Dreamer's Stance* (Ithaca, NY: Cornell U Press, 1965) 221, rightly asserts that "Eugene . . . hates Headstone for both his lower-class origins and his seriousness of purpose, which puts Eugene's frivolity to shame." And with the partial inadequacy of Lizzie in view, note this important statement made by Jennifer Gribble, in "Depth and Surface in *Our Mutual Friend*," *Essays in Criticism* 25 (1975): 203: "The bitter hostility between Eugene and Headstone begins to take on the aspect of a strange kinship . . . . Locked together in enmity, each draws from the other feelings and forces that neither of them has ever before recognized . . . . It is one of the most striking insights of the novel that Lizzie Hexam, ostensible cause of the men's rivalry, should fade into insignificance as the bizarre relationship between her two lovers develops. Although the novel clearly wishes to suggest that, for Eugene, the feelings brought alive in him by Lizzie at last create a more worthwhile self, it also strongly and more interestingly implies that such feelings, since they are usually ignored or suppressed, take on anarchic and perverted forms." Note that she implies a doubling effect between Bradley and Eugene.

[29.] P. 32.

> *Our Mutual Friend* is generally regarded as the most modern of
> Dickens's works because of the absence of a prominent omniscient
> voice and a clear omniscient perspective—the kind of voice and
> perspective we find in earlier novels such as *Bleak House* and *Little
> Dorrit.*[30]

And surely the most modern thing in the novel is the characterization of
Eugene, with his "urban anomie."[31] Eugene is open in the sense that he
disregards boundaries and conventions and is exploratory, and he is not
insofar as he depends excessively on guile, condescension, goading, and
deviousness.

Rogue Riderhood knows how to use guile, but he is more inclined to use
force. And that is the limitation on his openness. He tries to use force in
his attempt to have Gaffer Hexam indicted. He would be delighted to force
the steamer company to pay damages after the steamer hits his boat and
nearly causes his death. And he attempts to force Bradley to make blackmail
payments because Bradley ineptly imitates Rogue's clothing exactly when
he assaults Eugene. Manifestly, the wilfulness and the insistence on profit
in these ventures is hardly in line with the give and take which would be
a concomitant of real openness. To be sure, there is boldness in these
ventures just as there is boldness in Rogue's open willingness to venture
into Bradley's classroom and give us thereby one of the finest scenes in
the novel. Guile there may be in his talking over the heads of the boys,
but his message to Bradley is clear enough even if it is the use of coercion
on Bradley at the same time as it is a bold and open undertaking for this
ignorant but shrewd man.[32] There is a relative paucity of critical comment
on Rogue, but J. Fisher Solomon calls him "unredeemable,"[33] and in fact
Rogue is so unredeemable that he even takes what little money Betty
Higden has. The case of Rogue is perhaps even more complex than that

---

30. "Omniscience in *Our Mutual Friend*: On Taking the Reader by Surprise," *Journal of Narrative Technique* 17 (1987): 91.

31. Patrick O'Donnell, "'A Speeches of Chaff': Ventriloquy and Expression in *Our Mutual Friend*," *Dickens Studies Annual* 19 (1990): 268.

32. Note this statement of A. E. Dyson, in *The Inimitable Dickens* (London: Macmillan, 1970) 259: "Bradley is characteristically too self-preoccupied to see Riderhood clearly, and he makes the fatal error natural to him as a schoolmaster, of confusing illiteracy with slowness of mind."

33. "Realism, Rhetoric, and Reification: Or the Case of the Missing Detective in *Our Mutual Friend*," *Modern Philology* 86 (1988): 42.

of Eugene. One can be both open and decisive, and one can be decisive without the use of coercion. Rogue is then open and closed, but he is far more able to be open than Bradley.[34]

Absolute openness is of course an impossible ideal, particularly in an ambiance such as that of *Our Mutual Friend,* wherein "people become unnaturally watchful, uneasily conspiratorial."[35] Experience teaches us that there are times to say what one thinks, times to be silent, and even times to lie for the sake of one's own well-being or that of others. We also know that much we try to keep from others cannot be hidden despite our most careful efforts. With qualifications, then, openness is a positive quality, variously a show of trust which hopefully will be reciprocated by others, a recognition of necessity, and finally a means of psychic economy. The case of Bradley Headstone shows what self-crippling results from claustration, whether it is willed, a reflex act of self-defense, or some combination of both. The examples of Lizzie, Eugene, and Rogue show how openness can

---

[34] See again note 28. Stoehr says (pp. 222-23): "Obviously a violent criminal type, Riderhood represents one extreme on a continuum of passion and restraint, crime and law-abiding order, which runs from him through Headstone to Eugene . . . . The three characters represent the ambivalence in Dickens' feelings about law and order, crime and punishment. To borrow (and modify slightly) Riderhood's own version of their relations to each other, they stand for the 'one, t'other, and t'otherest' aspects of the same conflict between legality and crime." The problem in this important statement is to determine how "passion and restraint" are supposed to parallel "crime and law-abiding order." Suggestive but more useful with other Dickens characters, as the context admits, is the statement of Thomas Kelly, in "Character in Dickens' Late Novels," *Modern Language Quarterly* 30 (1969): 398: "What, we may ask, of the values that are set in motion by a certain degree of two-dimensional characterization? Dickens' frequent use of paired characters to simulate complex mental states, for example, demands personae who are individually flat. The method assumes a form of critical arithmetic: we perceive the flatness of a given character as a fraction which we are encouraged to add to some other fractional character in order to form an integer, a round figure." Kelly also says (again p. 398) that "In a true pair, the partners will represent discrete and opposed moral or psychic conditions."

[35] Gribble, p. 206. Another important feature of the novel is pointed out by O'Donnell (p. 267) when he speaks of "the rivalries between symbolic brothers or 'partners' (Headstone/Wrayburn, Riderhood/Gaffer, Harmon/Handford/ Rokesmith)." He should have added Radfoot/Harmon, Wegg/Boffin, and Headstone/Riderhood.

be liberating even as we note the ways in which openness is hedged about by elements of secrecy, guile, coercion, and sadism. When we enlarge the picture a bit, we notice that for various reasons Radfoot, Harmon-Handford-Rokesmith, Boffin, Wegg, Venus, the Lammles, Fledgeby, Riah, and others in the novel practice claustration. And though individual plans, foibles, problems, plots, and character flaws explain much of such claustration on an individual basis, they cumulatively are an indictment of the conditions, standards, and dysfunctions of the society depicted. The conclusion of the Harmon-Boffin-Wilfer plot may seem to suggest that a new era of openness is on the way, but we cannot base so general a conclusion on one situation, and we note that Eugene is cast out at the very end by the "voice of Society" (IV, xvii).[36] Claustration is aided and abetted by society. To live in a relatively open way is at the least a challenge. But to practice claustration to the extent Bradley Headstone does is so to retard growth that when one ventures at last into the larger world, the venture may prove to lead to self-destruction.

[36.] P. 796 in this edition of the novel.

V

NOTES FROM UNDERGROUND: THE BURIED LIFE

M ikhaïl Bakhtine says in his *La Poetique de Dostoïevski*:

> Dans l'esprit de la critique littéraire, l'art de Dostoïevski
> s'est décomposé en une suite de constructions philosophiques
> autonomes et contradictoires, défendues par les différents
> personnages. La conception philosophique de l'auteur y figure
> également, mais à une place tout a fait secondaire. Pour certains
> exégètes, la voix de Dostoïevski se confond avec celle de tel ou tel
> de ses personnages, pour d'autres, c'est une synthèse particulière
> de toutes ces voix idéologiques, pour d'autres enfin, elle est
> complètement recouverte par la voix des héros . . . .
>
> . . .
>
> *La pluralité des voix et des consciences indépendantes et distinctes,*
> *la polyphonie authentique des voix à part entière, constituent en effet un*
> *trait fondamental des romans de Dostoïevski* . . . . [1]

This polyphonic effect can be seen clearly in Dostoevsky's great novels,
but does it apply to *Notes from Underground* (*Zapiski iz podpol'ia*), with its
dominating speaker-protagonist who is never named? The effect may not
be as clear in *Notes*, but it is nonetheless there. Besides the views of the
underground man, we see in it the views of his former schoolmates, of
Apollon, and particularly of Liza as well as the unspoken but clear view
of the officer and the views of the "gentlemen" the underground man
addresses which he tries to anticipate. Thus there is dominance, if the

---

[1] Trans. Isabelle Kolitcheff (Paris: Éditions du Scuil, 1970), pp. 31 and 32.

86

underground man's dilemmas allow for it, but there is yet polyphony. Jacques Catteau, writing of *Notes*, supports this position: "Le locuteur est unique mais les voix sont multiples."[2] But where does *Notes* stand in relation to the great novels, *Crime and Punishment, The Possessed (The Devils) , The Idiot, The Brothers Karamazov,* where the polyphony is overpowering? *Notes* was written in 1864, before the great novels, and Donald Fanger says: "*Notes from Underground* is generally considered to inaugurate Dostoevsky's second and major period; but it does so by bringing to an end his first period."[3] Thus, aside from what *Notes* is in itself, it is a pivotal work. Warren Carrier states that it is a fragment[4] though it seems to end fittingly with the account of the underground man's botched relationship with Liza, but Dostoevsky brings it to an end by saying: "This is not the end, however, of the 'Notes' of this paradoxical writer. He could not help going on. But to us too it seems that this will be a good place to stop."[5] Ronald Hingley says of *Notes*:

> Here through his narrator, Dostoyevsky at last proclaims a thesis that was to dominate his later thinking and much of his greatest fiction: man is unpredictable, irrational, inconsistent, wayward and capricious. This was not a new discovery in itself, but its expression is highly original.[6]

This is all accurate enough except that the underground man, the representative man, becomes highly predictable. Paul F. Cardaci asserts that Dostoevsky created in the underground man a type, not an individual, and says further that he is a "symbol" for the general condition of educated Russians in the second half of the nineteenth century.[7] A type he is, but he is still highly individualized. Dostoevsky himself acknowledges the underground man's representative nature when he says at the very beginning:

2. *La Création littéraire chez Dostoïevski*, Bibliothèque russe de l'Institut d'études slaves, 49 (Paris: Institut d'études slaves, 1978), p. 114.
3. *Dostoevsky and Romantic Realism: A Study of Dostoevsky in Relation to Balzac, Dickens, and Gogol* (Cambridge, Mass.: Harvard Univ. Press, 1965), p. 177.
4. "Artistic Form and Unity in *Notes from the Underground*," *Renascence*, 16 (1964), 145.
5. Citations from Dostoevsky in my text are to *Notes from Underground*, in *Notes from Underground* and *The Double*, trans. Jessie Coulson (Harmondsworth, Engl.: Penguin, 1972). Here p. 123. Further page references are given in the text.
6. *Dostoyevsky: His Life and Work* (New York: Scribner, 1978), p. 101.
7. "Dostoevsky's Underground as Allusion and Symbol," *Symposium*, 28 (1974), 249.

> *The author of these Notes, and the Notes themselves, are both, of course,*
> *imaginary. All the same, if we take into consideration the conditions that*
> *have shaped our society, people like the writer not only may, but must,*
> *exist in that society . . . .* (p. 13)

The underground man's typicality is also stressed by James Holquist.[8] Joseph Frank, in the course of an expansive view on *Notes*, additionally sees the underground man as representative:

> if we are interested in understanding Dostoevsky's own point of view, so far as this can be reconstructed, then we must take it *[Notes]* for what it was initially meant to be—a brilliantly Swiftian satire, remarkable for the finesse of its conception and the brio of its execution, which dramatizes the dilemmas of a representative Russian personality attempting to live by the two European codes whose unhappy effects Dostoevsky explores.[9]

Satiric *Notes* undoubtedly is, but despite the satire I think Dostoevsky's relationship to the underground man needs to be explored, and further on I shall do so.

Notes is divided into two parts in which the chronological order is reversed. In Part I, a largely theoretical statement, the underground man's age is forty. In Part II, which is narrative, his age is twenty-four. He begins Part I by saying: "I am a sick man . . . . I am an angry man. I am an unattractive man. I think there is something wrong with my liver" (p. 15). He says that he respects doctors, but he won't go to a doctor. This is the first of a number of contradictions in him. Shortly afterwards he says that he is well-educated but still superstitious. It is said that the climate of St. Petersburg is bad for him, and it costs too much to live there, but he won't move. He says that the deeper he sank into his slime, the more aware he was of beauty. And he says that he takes pleasure in degradation. "'I'm sensitive and quick to take offence'" (p. 19), he says, but he adds that sometimes he might have been glad for a slap in the face. He gets pleasure from despair. He says that he isn't concerned about what the reader thinks, but he is often speculating on what the reader must be thinking. As an intelligent man he has to recognize the laws of nature, but he can't be reconciled to those

---

8. "Plot and Counter-Plot in *Notes from Underground*," *Canadian-American Slavic Studies*, 6 (1972), 236.

9. *Dostoevsky: The Stir of Liberation, 1860-1865* (Princeton, NJ: Princeton Univ. Press, 1986), p. 316.

laws. This is a major theme of Part I and will be dealt with separately. He says that he is joking but jokes with clenched teeth. Furthermore, he says that he doesn't believe what he's said, and then he turns around and says that he believes what he's said but suspects that he's lying like a trooper. This list shows how ambivalent he is and how easily he is pulled from one extreme to the other.

The other main theme in Part I besides the laws of nature is the position and dilemma of the intellectual. The underground man says first that too much thinking is a disease. And while too much thinking can impede one's ability to act, as he well knows, the condition of those who think little is not on the whole to be admired. He says further that every kind of intellectual activity is a disease, which is utterly false. The world would be in virtual darkness were it not for intellectual activity. Then he says directly that those who think don't act. This may be true of some, but for others John Dewey's statements that thinking is no more than assessing the possible effectiveness of planned actions are a guiding principle. He goes on to say that he is green with envy of spontaneous men even if they are stupid. This means of course that his own ability to act is impeded, but though he says he writes only out of boredom, his writing is an act to compensate for the actions he, because of his character and lack of opportunity, is unable to take. Next he says that the thinking man looks on himself as a mouse in relation to the man of action. He well may look on himself as a mouse, but he generalizes far too much. Finally he says that inertia, doing nothing, is best, but even he writes, and if otherwise he thinks inertia best, that is his problem. In all this he is starkly contrasting intellectuals, who supposedly see clearly but can't act, with the "normal" men who can act and, he holds, are stupid. Because someone is relatively unreflective and spontaneous doesn't necessarily mean that he is stupid, and, again, some intellectuals can and do act. Intellectuals are better contrasted to the masses who just read newspapers and murder mysteries and, in our century, watch television, people who are not to be esteemed and whose actions are often likely to be stupid. But the dichotomy of the intellectual who purportedly can't act and the stupid man of action is patently false.

The underground man has high intellectual powers, but he has a mind that is perverse not in a positive sense but in a wrongheaded sense. He has to recognize the laws of nature though emotionally he cannot accept them. But he is simply wrong to say that man is held to be descended from the ape when Darwin said only that man is a primate, hence related to the ape. One thing he particularly takes exception to is the fact that two plus two equals four. He says that two plus two equals five is also a fine thing. I see no reason to object to two plus two equals four, and his rebellion against it seems merely silly and childish. He also says that for one's best one must go against all laws, and while this sounds healthily anarchic, to go against the laws of nature is utter folly and a way to harm oneself, but then he is a masochist, for he says that self-flagellation is stimulating. He values his will, and science says that man acts by the laws of nature. But he is wrong to think that willful acts, the acts of capriciousness he so values, are free because even they are determined. He points out that many people have perversely pursued difficult paths, but this shows principally that he, as a masochist, has a lot of company. And he points out the widespread phenomenon of warfare and bloodshed and the irrationality of world history, but these things only show how few men act humanely and rationally. He sees, with the strong influx of science in his time, it coming to this: all will be plotted mathematically, all problems will vanish, and the Crystal Palace will arise. This view is fatuously optimistic though not of course optimistic to the underground man, and science, in the face of widespread human irrationality, has of course limited efficacy to do positive things. But here we come to the underground man's reading. There was a Crystal Palace near London which burned in the twentieth century and has perhaps been rebuilt, but it was used as a metaphor by a particular author. Frank, among others, identifies this author and the work in question:

> The outstanding spokesman for the Russian radicals at this moment [of the publication of *Notes*] was Nicolai G. Chernyshevsky, whose Utopian novel *What Is To Be Done?* had appeared in the spring of 1863 and had caused a sensation. *Notes from Underground* was intended as an answer to *What Is To Be Done?*; and the accepted account of the relation between them runs as follows.
>
> Chernyshevsky and the radicals believed that man was innately good and amenable to reason, and that, once enlightened as to his true interests, reason and science would ultimately enable him to construct a perfect society. Dostoevsky, on the other hand, believed that man was innately evil, irrational, capricious and destructive; not reason but only faith in Christ could ever succeed in helping him to master the chaos of his impulses . . . . [R]egardless of the differing explanations offered for the genesis of Dostoevsky's *Weltanschauung*, this interpretation of *Notes from Underground* has continued to reign unchallenged since.[10]

---

10. "Nihilism and *Notes from Underground*," *Sewanee Review*, 69 (1961), 2.

Neither Chernyshevsky nor Dostoevsky is right; man is neither good nor evil but a potential to be either vicious or humane. Freud discovered the death instinct in man,[11] and that phenomenon posits some sado-masochistic behavior in everyone. In the twentieth century scientific-technological reason has become so prevalent and oppressive it turns irrational. The reign of benign reason will never come. And the Crystal Palace is a mere ideal almost as flimsy as religious ideals.[12] The underground man need not fear not being allowed to stick out his tongue at the Crystal Palace. Dostoevsky, through his underground man, was not only protesting against science per se but surely also against particularly oppressive products of the scientific mind such as utilitarianism and positivism. And, late in the twentieth century, we have to contend with the especially oppressive spread of technology. But reason and science in their best tradition, which includes orthodox Freudian psychoanalysis, are to be honored.

A number of critics make observations bearing particularly on Part I. Malcolm V. Jones informs us that "The first part of *Notes from Underground* is the better known and is occasionally published on its own in the West."[13] Mark Spilka says:

> He [the underground man] has shown how the conclusions of scientific determinism subvert belief in human dignity and morality, reduce man to an organ-stop, a thing, in the name of rational abstractions, and he has opposed these conclusions with his own belief in free choice, in conscious and deliberate perversity, even when it leads to suffering.[14]

The best traditions of rationalism allow for a belief in human dignity, but in the interest of sexual freedom "morality" has to go. Sacvan Bercovitch underlines a point I made earlier: "Unwittingly he [the underground man] reveals himself . . . to be the spokesman for a rigid determinism: his 'free choice' rests in every case upon a false alternative."[15] Earl A. Cash says accurately enough:

11. See his *Beyond the Pleasure Principle*, trans. and newly ed. James Strachey (New York: Norton, 1961), passim.
12. According to Frank (*Dostoevsky*, p. 331): "The underground man . . . clings to his ideal of a 'true' Crystal Palace because of 'some old-fashioned, irrational habits of my generation.'"
13. *Dostoyevsky: The Novel of Discord* (London: Paul Elek, 1976), p. 56.
14. "Playing Crazy in the Underground," *Minnesota Review*, 6 (1966), 235.
15. "Dramatic Irony in *Notes from the Underground*," *Slavic and East European Journal*, 8 (1964), 285.

"the speaker in *Notes from Underground* is not to be dismissed as an imposter. He . . . runs into brick walls which genuinely distress him."[16] Carrier says:

> A recent critic has characterized Parts One and Two of *Notes from Underground* as "disjunct," Part Two being presented as the really crucial and valuable part of the novel . . . .
> A description of the relationship between Parts One and Two as that of "idea" and "illustration" is perhaps somewhat artificial and inaccurate, yet not without point. A better terminology might be "presentation" and "dramatic incident."[17]

Part II, being narrative, also seems to me the more valuable part of the novella. Carrier's attempt to relate the two parts is not totally satisfactory because Part I and II are in important ways concerned with different issues. Cardaci disagrees with what I've just said, but at any rate he is right on target as to the causation of the underground man's philosophy:

> Because his arguments in Part I are the direct result of his personal experience in Part II, the underground man's philosophy can never really be adequately treated independently of its psychological and sociological determinants.[18]

Holquist, in saying that Part I is merely talk and that Part II gives the lie to it,[19] makes an important statement but is being just slightly reductive. Michele Frucht Levy says incisively:

> As Part I ends, the Underground Man reflects on the "literary form" of his *Notes* . . . . In fact, despite his protestations to the contrary, he has always served form over content and goal over process, a choice which dooms him, even by his own logic, to inauthenticity and impotence.[20]

---

16. "The Narrators in *Invisible Man* and *Notes from Underground*: Brothers in the Spirit," *College Language Association Journal*, 16 (1973), 507. Ellison's invisible man is very sympathetic, but the underground man, except at points, I do not find sympathetic.
17. Pp. 142-43.
18. P. 248.
19. P. 227.
20. "D. H. Lawrence and Dostoevsky: The Thirst for Risk and the Thirst for Life," *Modern Fiction Studies*, 33 (1987), 283.

The boringly sermonizing David M. McKinney says:

> This portrayal of the Underground Man as a *man-god* attains its
> ultimate depiction when, not content merely to defy God, he yearns
> to supplant His very position as Creator. This Russian Prometheus
> would that all laws were subject to man, not God, and that man
> himself were responsible for these laws . . . .
>
> The Underground Man is humbled, however, in the enfeebling
> realization that he is not above God and His laws; he cannot penetrate
> beyond the walls of humanity, and in light of this painful impotency
> he regards himself as a "Mouse" ("mysh"). In his humiliation he
> can only slide back into his underground hole of inertia, crushed
> with the awareness of his human limitations . . . . [21]

This hysterical and out-of-focus statement is caught in the illusion that there
is a "God" to defy. The underground man is a theist of sorts, as he mentions
"God" three times in the course of the work, but obviously he hasn't found
the freedom from alienation which Dostoevsky assumed a belief in Jesus
would supply.[22] But William J. Leatherbarrow informs us that

> Dostoevsky intended at the end of Part I to advocate Christian
> faith as a means of attaining moral freedom without falling into
> the trap of consciousness, but his design was frustrated by the
> intervention of the censor, who balked at the thought of Gospel
> passages emanating from this hero's profaned lips . . . . [23]

The work, I firmly believe, is better without it.

Part II, the narrative of the underground man's youth, records that
"Even then my life was gloomy, untidy, and barbarously solitary" (p. 47).
He discusses first his relations with his fellow employees. These were always
uneasy, and at least at times he regarded the others as sheep. Finally he felt
indifference and skepticism and reproached himself with romanticism, and
here the text returns to the theoretical orientation of Part I briefly. After

---

[21.] *"Notes from Underground*: A Dostoevskean *Faust," Canadian-American Slavic Studies,*
12 (1978), 196.

[22.] See Isadore Traschen, "Existential Ambiguities in *Notes from Underground," South
Atlantic Quarterly,* 73 (1974), 374.

[23.] *Fedor Dostoevsky,* Twayne's World Authors Series, 636 (Boston: Twayne, 1981), pp.
67-68. See also Gary Rosenshield, "The Fate of Dostoevsky's Underground Man:
The Case for an Open Ending," *Slavic and East European Journal,* 28 (1984), 324.

saying that he finally became friends with his fellow employees (friendships which he didn't keep up), he expands to say that Russians are generally not "stupid transcendental romantics" (p. 49) of the German or French kind. Russian romantics, he maintains, are clearsighted but keep the "highest and best" (p. 50) within themselves. And yet he goes on to say that the Russian romantic is a man of the "widest sympathies" *and* a "supreme scoundrel" (p. 50). He is a scoundrel and yet devoted to ideals, which isn't, after all, so surprising. His remarks on Russian romantics are interesting, but the thing to notice here is the influx of romanticism from the West, a force paralleling the force of scientism on the older underground man. Frank says:

> The second part of *Notes from Underground* . . . is intended to satirize the sentimental social Romanticism of the Forties [e.g., of George Sand, Eugène Sue, and Victor Hugo] just as the first part had satirized the Nihilism of the Sixties. And a good deal of light is thrown on this second part by articles that Dostoevsky published in his magazine *Time* in the years immediately preceding the composition of his novella. The Forties, Dostoevsky wrote in 1860, had been the moment when "the spirit of analysis penetrated into our intellectual classes . . . . Then everything was done according to principle, we lived according to principles, and we had a horrible fear of doing anything not according to the latest ideas." All spontaneity and unselfconsciousness was lost; not to live by the light of "the latest ideas" was literally unthinkable. And under the influence of "the latest ideas" a new social type appeared among the Russian intelligentsia—the "Byronic natures," the liberal idealists of the Forties.[24]

It is a bit hard, in the light of what follows in Part II, to know how to apply this to the underground man until one lights on a sentence a bit farther in Frank's discussion:

> The social Romanticism of the Forties, in Dostoevsky's opinion, had fostered an inflated "egoism of principle," which allowed the Russian intelligentsia to live in a dream-world of "universal" beneficence while actually nursing their own vanity with perfect moral complacency.[25]

[24.] "Nihilism," p. 24.

[25.] P. 25. See also Traschen, p. 367, and Richard Peace, *Dostoyevsky: An Examination of the Major Novels* (Cambridge: Cambridge Univ. Press, 1971), p. 5.

The ideal of "'universal' beneficence" doesn't apply too well to the underground man, but an "'egoism of principle,'" immense vanity, and dreams do. And then romanticism was intrinsically idealistic, and the underground man has his ideals, many of which are crushed for him by hard realities, but the ideal of something beyond the underground persists in him.

His vanity, or narcissism, is obviously intimately engaged in the extended plan to get revenge on the officer who bumped into him without deigning even to notice him. That he cannot simply forget this incident shows how hypersensitive and touchy he is. He meets the officer often in the street, and especially on Nevsky Prospect, and goes on in his rage for years, still planning revenge. He decides that his clothes are too shabby, gets a loan for new clothes from his boss, and finally collides with the officer's shoulder and so can get on to other dilemmas. Richard Weisberg speaks here generally, but his statement has direct bearing on this sequence in the underground man's life: "The 'ressentient' man lives through, again and again, the event which has rendered him bitter and revealed his impotence . . . ."[26] Frank informs us that both bumping into the officer and the encounter with Liza are parodies of incidents in Chernyshevsky's *What Is To Be Done?*[27] And Rudolph Neuhäuser points out that "The theme of social inequality was illustrated in the story of the Underground Man's collision with the unnamed officer . . . ."[28] This theme is continued in the account of the dinner with the underground man's old schoolfellows.

The underground man had been getting out, aside from going to his job, to frequent prostitutes, for he informs us that he was sickened at the end of periods of what he calls dissipation. He also sometimes visits his boss, Anton Antonovich. Then he has further social urges and goes to see his old schoolfellow Simonov, with whom are two other old schoolfellows, after almost a year. Simonov is astonished that he has come, and he is ignored. It happens that the next evening there is a farewell dinner for Zverkov, another old schoolmate. Zverkov, now successful as an army officer, had been a poor student, he is good looking, and the underground man had hated him for his "social dexterity" and "good manners" (p. 63) and probable future

---

26. "An Example Not to Follow,: *Ressentiment* and the Underground Man," *Modern Fiction Studies*, 21 (1975), 555.

27. *Dostoevsky*, p. 313.

28. "Observations on the Structure of *Notes from Underground* with Reference to the Main Themes of Part II," *Canadian-American Slavic Studies*, 6 (1972), 245.

successes with women. The underground man, enraged that Simonov knows he doesn't really want to go to the dinner, feels he needn't go but knows he'll go. At the dinner he suffers under Zverkov's "lofty and condescending politeness" (p. 72) and his own "lack of social experience" (p. 73). Trudolyubov initially sticks up for him but soon turns against him. After being obliged to tell his salary, which is termed pitiful, he is again ignored, thinks of going but stays, gets very drunk as his anger grows. The others worship Zverkov. Then the others leave, and he is alone. Here, and to a degree with his fellow employees, he is a sympathetic character. He is manifestly ill-treated by his old schoolfellows. He had earlier suffered in school, being shy and introspective and an orphan sent there by "distant and indifferent relations."[29] The underground man had long owed Simonov fifteen roubles, and on the evening of the dinner he again borrows money from Simonov. Bercovitch notes that Simonov had never asked for repayment,[30] but despite that Simonov's treatment of him is shabby. Bercovitch also sees good qualities in Zverkov,[31] but Zverkov is simply a man without real qualities destined to succeed. The underground man wants, on the evening of the dinner, to duel Zverkov, and Roger B. Anderson comments accurately on his "stylized dream of romantic revenge . . . ."[32] Neuhäuser says:

> An unwillingness to recognize social reality, coupled with a desire to succeed within the existing order, an escape into vice as a substitute reality, disguised by a feigned belief in romantic-idealistic notions—these were the main characteristics of many educated young men of the 1840's of the type of Zverkov and his friends.[33]

Neuhäuser is being moralistic in speaking of "vice," but otherwise his summary is accurate enough. Frank observes that with these men he wants esteem and gets distancing.[34] After the dinner the underground man of course goes to a brothel, and Bernard J. Paris rightly comments that "His initial impulse is, of course, aggressive; he restores his pride, after the

---

[29]. Fanger, p. 179.
[30]. P. 287.
[31]. Again, p. 287.
[32]. *Dostoevsky: Myths of Duality* (Gainesville: Univ. of Florida Press, 1986), p. 40.
[33]. P. 246.
[34]. *Dostoevsky*, p. 339.

humiliations of the dinner, through sexual mastery and by successfully playing upon Liza's feelings."[35]

As he is in bed with her, he observes: "I saw two eyes . . . . Their look was coldly indifferent, sullen, like something utterly alien; it irked me . . . ." (p. 86). He now first speaks to her. He tells Liza "sadistically" (p. 89) what is perhaps true but what of course he ought not to say: in another year she'll be in a poorer house, in yet another year she'll be in an even poorer house, and finally she'll be in a cellar in the Haymarket. (When he tells her later that in the Haymarket she'll be beaten, she bites her hands till the blood comes.) He says that he may wallow in filth but is nobody's slave, whereas she is a slave, and it will be harder and harder for her to get out of her slavery. Martin P. Rice, comparing Hegel's master-and-slave concept with Dostoevsky's *Notes*, comments on the underground man's getting mastery over Liza:

> By the time the Underground Man is ready to leave Liza, it seems that for once in his life he has successfully established himself as master in the struggle of the first self-consciousness with the other. Liza has been reduced to a state that might be compared to non-existence, certainly to dependence . . . .

[35.] "*Notes from Underground*: A Horneyan Analysis," *PMLA*, 88 (1973), 516. Paris's Horneyan analysis, in brief, runs thus:

> Under unfavorable conditions, when the people around him are prevented by their own neurotic needs from relating to him with love and respect, the child develops a "feeling of being isolated and helpless in a world conceived as potentially hostile" . . . . This feeling of "basic anxiety" makes the child fearful of spontaneity, and, forsaking his real self, he develops neurotic strategies for coping with his environment.
>
> These strategies are of three kinds: the individual can adopt the self-effacing or compliant solution and move toward people; he can develop the aggressive or expansive solution and move against people; or he can become detached or resigned and move away from people (p. 511).

According to Paris, one of these trends is emphasized with resultant conflicts, and the other possible trends are condemned and suppressed (p. 512). Paris rightly sees the underground man's choice as detachment (p. 513), but the marked aggressive traits in him should be noted. Karen Horney was a Neo-Freudian, and while Neo-Freudianism should be avoided because it detaches itself from Freud's *bodily* base, the above analysis at any rate seems helpful.

But Rice goes on to point out that

> what the Underground Man soon discovers is that his is a dependent
> consciousness because he depends on the unessential consciousness,
> the slave Liza, for his essential consciousness to exist. He has no
> independent existence without the consciousness of the slave.[36]

The underground man doesn't leave Liza yet. He talks for a time sentimentally of love. Liza has now become gentle and shy, and she observes that he speaks "like a book" (p. 95). But he resumes his sadistic talk. After he has finished, she shows him a declaration of love given her by a medical student who didn't know that she was in a brothel. Scott Consigny sees Liza finding an image of herself through the letter,[37] and this may well be so, but he makes that fit his mistaken thesis that "Because there is no independent reality beyond our textual portrayals, it is an illusion to believe that we can live without texts, 'immediately' or 'directly.'"[38] The underground man has given Liza his address and asked her to visit him but afterwards dreads that she actually will come.

She does come just as he is quarreling with his servant Apollon. Zola's servants in *Pot-Bouille* are healthily contemptuous of their employers, but Apollon is just intolerable. Perhaps in part as compensation for being only a servant, he shows contempt and condescension to the underground man, and he is condescending with everyone. He is very pedantic, has inordinate self-esteem, does almost nothing, and tyrannizes his master, but the underground man, who hates him, finds it impossible to turn him out. Liza, seeing the quarrel, is confused. The underground man sends Apollon out for tea and rusks, and then he cries, becomes hysterical, feels shame, and feels rage against Liza. He, who had the upper hand at the brothel, is now seen by her in abject misery. She says that she wants to leave the brothel and is obviously seeking his help to do so. But he says that he was laughing at her, is laughing at her, and was taking revenge on her because of the treatment of him at the dinner. She turns white and is crushed by his remarks. He says that he wanted power and that it was the "fascination of the game" (p. 116). After reviling himself, he says that he won't forgive her. Liza feels love for him, understands more than he thinks she does, and sees that he's unhappy. She considers herself beneath him, comes timidly

---

36. "Dostoevskii's *Notes from Underground* and Hegel's 'Master and Slave,'" *Canadian-American Slavic Studies*, 8 (1974), 365-66.

37. "The Paradox of Textuality: Writing as Entrapment and Deliverance in *Notes from the Underground*," *Canadian-American Slavic Studies*, 12 (1978), 342.

38. P. 347.

and puts her arms around him, and both cry. He says, as a child might, "'I'm incapable of being . . . good!'" (p. 117). There are more hysterics, he at the same time hates her and is attracted to her, and she knows that he's not in a condition to love her. He now considers himself stupid. Love to him means being tyrannical and holding the moral upper hand. Thus, all conflicts aside, he doesn't know what love is. Finally Liza leaves, and the underground man never sees nor hears of her again.

Quite a number of critics have commented on the episodes with Liza, but three of them will be dealt with first because they bring up crucial issues about these episodes. Nicholas Moravcevich says:

> ultimately his own work /Dostoevsky's/ retains much of that sentimental undertone that bothered him in the works of the contemporary liberals, since the grossly deceived and insulted Liza (whose trustfulness and naïveté are deliberately highlighted so that her antagonist can trample on them) ultimately emerges so exalted that she herself readily becomes a new romantic symbol of the fallen woman, this one of Dostoevskij's own making.
>
> In fact, this is doubly true, for Liza appears to be just as much a character of the underground man's own making, since she is wholly his invention . . . .[39]

Gary Rosenshield says: "His /the underground man's/ salvation would come—if it did at all—through the acceptance and appreciation of the ideal of compassion and self-sacrifice embodied in the prostitute Liza . . . ."[40] And Frank relatedly says that Liza's "selfless" love is a way out for the underground man and that she embodies a Christian ideal.[41] There well may be elements of the nineteenth-century sentimentalization of the prostitute in Liza's portrayal, though she is certainly far more believable than the pious and incredibly innocent Sonia of *Crime and Punishment*, and Dostoevsky may well have intended her to embody a Christian ideal. But what none of these critics, nor any whose views are to follow, pounces upon is the fact that Liza is a very young girl who has been in the brothel only two weeks, and at the time of her visit to the underground man only two weeks and several days. Initially hard and cold, she shortly reverts to her girlish, pre-brothel warmth and capability for feeling. She comes to love the underground man, and even when she sees that he, because of his torn and

---

[39]. "The Romantization of the Prostitute in Dostoevskij's Fiction," *Russian Literature*, NS 4 (1976), 302.

[40]. P. 325.

[41]. *Dostoevsky*, pp. 344 and 346.

suffering condition, cannot take her in, she still feels strongly towards and about him. There is compassion in her, and she comes to see that she has nothing to gain, and in this there is her girlish warmth resurgent after a very short time in the brothel. I think that Liza is believable and existent apart from the underground man, but I see why these critics make the statements they do.

The remaining critics say various things. Spilka says:

> The reality which he /the underground man / grasps, but fails to hold, is Liza. This unusual prostitute is like him in important ways: a cold lover, an indifferent watcher during intercourse and after; cynical about life, death, marriage; analytically keen; and secretly romantic.[42]

This statement is accurate only in part; Liza is not really cynical, and she shows the capacity to be a warm lover. Bercovitch says of Liza: "The shy and bewildered girl overcomes her humiliation in compassionate recognition of the other's suffering."[43] Carrier pointedly notes that "His /the underground man's/ rejection of her /Liza/ is the ultimate rejection of himself."[44] Holquist says: "Dostoevskii has dramatized a contrast between Nekrasov's sentimental version of the prostitute and his own realistic picture,"[45] thus implicitly or explicitly disagreeing with Moravcevich, Rosenshield, and Frank. Isadore Traschen comments not on Liza but on the underground man in relation to her as he says: "With only a spiteless spite, unable to love, he compensates through power, which only intensifies his alienation."[46] Robert Louis Jackson approaches the positions of Rosenshield and Frank as he says that Liza shows "Christian love and self-sacrifice . . . ."[47] There is no indication that Liza is a Christian, and I prefer to see her actions as simply compassionate, not self-sacrificial. Weisberg sees in Liza's leaving the money that the underground man has given her her "moral superiority"[48] to him. And finally Alex de Jonge, a bit redundantly, terms the underground man's telling Liza her probable fate "sexual sadism."[49]

---

42. P. 237.
43. P. 289.
44. P. 144.
45. P. 229. Two lines from Nekrasov are quoted twice in *Notes*.
46. P. 370.
47. "Aristotelian Movement and Design in Part Two of *Notes from the Underground*," in *Dostoevsky: New Perspectives*, ed. Robert Louis Jackson (Englewood Cliffs, NJ: Prentice-Hall, 1984), p. 67.
48. P. 563.
49. *Dostoevsky and the Age of Intensity* (New York: St. Martin's Press, 1975), pp. 184-85.

There is a great variety of opinions on the underground man, as we see him in Parts I and II, among the critics. Ruth Mortimer moralistically says that "The self-willed, self-incriminating underground man is the embodiment of evil, the prototype of the sensualists, the relativists, the nihilists in the later novels."[50] Neuhäuser reiterates a point made earlier with these remarks:

> As long as the Underground Man remains in the magic circle of sentimental-romantic-idealistic concepts, he will have nothing more positive to offer than an irrational, illusory freedom of will based on a hypertrophic egotism—since this is the only reality in the underground.[51]

Joseph Beatty says that "the UM's [underground man's] suffering is generated by his desire for holistic self-expression in conjunction with his recognition that he is always other than his expressions."[52] J. R. Hall, like Neuhäuser, touches on a point previously made:

> Speaking of a perverse pleasure in being slapped, the Underground Man relates this example of his masochism to a generalization already established, namely that a certain kind of pleasure consists in the contemplation of the self as subject to inevitable laws . . . .[53]

Traschen says: "*in actual, concrete instances this exemplar of freedom* [the underground man] *is enslaved by conventional language and emotions.*" He adds further on that "he fears real life" and says "he cannot love."[54] Carrier rightly suggests that "he [the underground man] is in a condition of *stasis.*"[55] Cash says of him:

> From . . . [a given passage] and kindred fantasies, the reader might begin to perceive the undergrounder for the romantic

---

50. "Dostoevski and the Dream," *Modern Philology*, 54 (1956), 106.
51. P. 253.
52. "From Rebellion and Alienation to Salutary Freedom: A Study in *Notes from Underground*," *Soundings*, 61 (1978), 203.
53. "Abstraction in Dostoyevsky's *Notes from the Underground*," *Modern Language Review*, 76 (1981), 131.

54. Pp. 368, 389, and 370.
55. P. 143.

sap he is—captivated by his own histrionics and infatuated with his sometime bravura eloquence. No wonder he can revel in boredom, half expecting relief in writing.[56]

Spilka strikes a positive note in saying that "The underground man's assertive and emotive powers are confirmed . . . as sources of identity, personality, individuality."[57] He is certainly assertive, but he is as clearly emotionally confused. Thomas M. Kavanagh speaks generally, but at least the last part of his statement applies well to the underground man:

> Action becomes frenzy. Every movement, every contact with reality becomes an exercise in futility because it must abrogate not only the condemnation by the other, but the far more annihilating condemnation of the self by the self . . . .[58]

Reed Merrill asserts that "His /the underground man's/ suspicion of mankind's sacred ideals has led him to negate everything, especially himself, and his alternative to the stalemate of multiple zero is to withdraw from life, a moral cripple."[59] There is nothing sacred about mankind's illusory ideals. In answer to a question which he poses earlier, Paris says:

> We begin to see . . . the way in which the underground man's contradictory trends result in inconsistencies. His detachment leads him to scorn success, but his aggressive needs make him force his way to the top.[60]

He is on top only with Liza, and at that only in their first encounter. Cardaci rightly observes that

> Nowhere in the *Notes*, in fact, does the narrator show any real concern for anyone but himself. Unlike later underground types like Raskolnikov, Kirilov, and Ivan Karamazov who attempt

---

[56.] P. 506.

[57.] P. 242.

[58.] "Dostoyevsky's *Notes from Underground*: The Form of the Fiction," *Texas Studies in Literature and Language*, 14 (1972), 496. Kavanagh's insistence that *Notes* not be read psychologically (see p. 493) is utterly wrong.

[59.] "The Mistaken Endeavor: Dostoevsky's *Notes from the Underground*," *Modern Fiction Studies*, 18 (1972-73), 506.

[60.] P. 514.

to justify their actions because of conditions in Russia, the narrator's only real justification for his irrational behavior is the deep-seated, personal malice he believes every conscious human being possesses.[61]

Holquist says: "In the closing lines of the *Notes*, the meaning of the Underground Man's literariness is made explicit. He presents himself as *typical* of modern man: 'we have all lost touch with life . . . .'"[62] That is unfortunately only too true. Michael Haltresht is being absurd when he says:

> By their filthiness, furtiveness, fecundity, and destructiveness, rats serve to represent the narrator's irrepressible sexual drives—his homosexual propensities, his sadism . . . , his joyless contacts with prostitutes, and such other unnamed "ugly" "actions that all, perhaps, commit" . . . .[63]

Consigny is only stating the obvious when he says: "The underground man learns, in his underground, that to keep silent is to retreat from life rather than to experience it more fully."[64] Terrence Doody seems to be advocating solipsism when he says:

> Like Rousseau, the Underground Man is motivated by the crisis of his isolation. But in the polemic he never treats it as a crisis; he treats it as an advantage for the superior insight it affords.[65]

Barbara F. Howard observes the underground man's exaggerated fear of reader response and that in him a "romantic dreamer" and "sentimental misanthrope" are fused.[66] Rosenshield is being sublimely optimistic when he says: "Dostoevsky does not leave the Underground Man without hope

---

[61.] P. 249.

[62.] P. 236.

[63.] "Symbolism of Rats and Mice in Dostoevsky's *Notes from the Underground*," *South Atlantic Bulletin*, 39, No. 4 (1974), 60.

[64.] P. 349.

[65.] "The Underground Man's Confession and His Audience," *Rice University Studies*, 61, No. 1 (1975), 30.

[66.] "The Rhetoric of Confession: Dostoevsky's *Notes from Underground* and Rousseau's *Confessions*," *Slavic and East European Journal*, 25, No. 4 (1981), 20 and 24.

of resolving his philosophical, moral, and psychological difficulties and of eventually experiencing spiritual regeneration."[67] Frank observes that

> In fact, the underground man is shown as being caught in a conflict between the egoistic aspects of his character and the sympathetic, outgoing ones that he also posseses [sic]; but these latter are continually suppressed in favor of the former.[68]

J. Middleton Murry, in speaking of the underground man's "taste for ugly debauchery,"[69] is both being moralistic and ignoring the underground man's feelings about frequenting prostitutes. Anderson compares him to Golyadkin in (Dostoevsky's) *The Double* but correctly notes that Golyadkin is "essentially . . . *[a]* passive victim."[70] Anderson also aligns the underground man with the trickster figure, especially in Part II.[71] R. Causinos-Assens also compares the underground man with Golyadkin but doesn't make the necessary distinction that Anderson does.[72] De Jonge elaborates on a point made earlier:

> The Underground Man is a masochist of a subtler and more perverse kind *[than Marmeladov of Crime and Punishment]*. One of his characteristics, one which is positively Baudelairian, is his ability to turn his sense of remorseful self-disgust into a source of pleasure.[73]

Janko Lavrin has an assessment of the underground man which is harsh even considering his many difficulties: "Too weak to cope with life and its 'laws', he has become a failure, a nobody, whom people can insult as they like."[74] Jones is hardly breaking new ground when he points to the underground man's "underlying malice and resentment . . . ."[75] Jackson calls him "amoral," "compulsive," and reactive."[76] Rado Pribic says:

---

[67] P. 324.
[68] *Dostoevsky*, p. 317.
[69] *Fyodor Dostoevsky: A Critical Study* (New York: Russell & Russell, 1966), p. 93.
[70] P. 28.
[71] P. 44. See Paul Radin's *The Trickster: A Study in American Indian Mythology* (New York: Schocken, 1972), passim, on the Winnebago trickster figure.
[72] *Fiodor Mijailovich Dostoyevski: el novelista de lo subconsciente* (Madrid: M. Aguilar, n.d.), p. 31 et passim.
[73] P. 171.
[74] *Dostoevsky: A Study* (New York: Macmillan, 1947), p. 65.
[75] P. 65.
[76] P. 70.

The underground man painfully senses the disparity between his character and its manifestation under given circumstances, but he goes on destroying his emotions with his intellect and annihilating his rational considerations with his whimsical will.[77]

And finally, though Jackson mentions the underground man's compulsiveness in passing, Barbara Smalley devotes an entire and excellent article to this trait of his. Particular note should be taken of this statement:

> The underground man's reactions are, of course, more complex than this outline of them [above] allows for. A part of him is not involved in the hatred and is appalled at the cunning and cruelty of the other part of him that it is helpless to restrain .... [H]e stops short in his pursuit [of Liza], realizing that he is helpless to prevent habitual patterns from governing his conduct, even if he should catch up with her .... [78]

With some exceptions which are off base, the critics on the whole do a good and annihilating job in summing up the underground man. But no critic I have consulted seems to see that he is a paranoid schizophrenic. Schizophrenia is, technically, a problem in keeping subject and object separate or distinct, but in its more commonly known aspect it is a divided personality. The underground man may well have problems of reference, but quite obviously he is a divided personality.

Notes is of course a confession, and the underground man explicitly links it to an earlier confession:

> Heine states that trustworthy autobiographies are almost an impossibility, and that a man will probably never tell the truth about himself. According to him Rousseau, for example, lied about himself in his *Confessions*, even deliberately, out of vanity. I am sure Heine was right .... (p. 45)

---

77. "*Notes from the Underground*: One Hundred Years After the Author's Death," in *Dostoevsky and the Human Condition After a Century*, ed. Alexej Ugrinsky, Contributions to the Study of World Literature, no. 16 (New York: Greenwood, 1986), p. 73.
78. "The Compulsive Patterns of Dostoyevsky's Underground Man," *Studies in Short Fiction*, 10 (1973), 395. See passim, pp. 389-96.

Paul Green

The underground man is also vain or narcissistic, and he is often not sure whether he is telling the truth or lying. At any rate, Dostoevsky had Rousseau in mind in writing *Notes*, but prior to Rousseau is of course Augustine. René E. Fortin says of Augustine's writings:

> The confession which emerges from Augustine embodies formal elements which will henceforth characterize the genre: first, the problematic nature of the narratorial "I," who is present in the work as at once exploring subject and explored object . . . ; secondly, the narrator's intricate relationship with his audience, the readers whom he needs to fulfill the design of the confession.[79]

And of the underground man in relation to Augustine, Fortin says:

> the narrator of *Notes from Underground* . . . is a composite of Rousseau and Augustine, a Rousseauvian narrator struggling mightily to escape from the trap of Rousseauvian form—with its implicit values—and to gain the high ground of the Augustinian confession that would make him whole.[80]

But did Augustine's Christianity really make him "whole," and how can we be sure that he also didn't do some lying? So much for Augustine; the underground man's relationship to Rousseau merits more attention. Fortin says further:

> It is this mutated form of the confession /confession as apologia/ that Dostoyevsky inherits and re-shapes for his own distinct purposes, creating a work that may be seen as part parody and part imitation of the Rousseauvian confession.[81]

Being more specific, Fortin says:

> The *Notes* . . . may be seen as Dostoyevsky's answer to Rousseau. Rejecting the values of Rousseau—in particular, the pelagianism that underlies his concept of the natural man—the narrator

---

[79]. "Responsive Form: Dostoyevsky's *Notes from Underground* and the Confessional Tradition," *Essays in Literature*, 7 (1980), 226.
[80]. P. 225.
[81]. P. 234.

106

frantically struggles to discover the form of confession that would be truest to man's situation in the nineteenth century. But since the narrator cannot exorcise his personal demons, his confession falls short, and he must grudgingly admit his kinship with Rousseau.[82]

Rousseau has as good a claim as any modern man to be the father of romanticism, and Fortin goes on to say: "The Rousseauvian elements in the *Notes* are unmistakable. Part of the narrator's burden of guilt consists of his Rousseauvian past, his intoxication with the heady wine of romanticism"[83] Two other critics also comment on the relationship of *Notes* to Rousseau's *Confessions*. Doody's statement about the underground man, Rousseau, and the crisis of isolation has been quoted above. Howard says:

> the Underground Man points to an essential difference between his notion of confession and Rousseau's; namely, his belief that, as M. Holquist puts it, "the form of biography is always false to the essence of the life it tells." That is to say, in confession there is an irreconcilable rift between form and substance.[84]

Augustine and Rousseau wrote about their lives, and Dostoevsky gives us the confession of a fictional character, but Dostoevsky held that people like his underground man must have existed in the Russia of his time.

What is the relationship of Dostoevsky to his underground man? A number of critics have supplied comments on this topic. Bercovitch sees a close relation: "his *[*the underground man's*]* 'confession' is said to embody the liberty of the human spirit, to represent Dostoevsky's archetypal-autobiographical answer to mechanized society."[85] Edward Wasiolek says something in part analogous:

> The Underground Man is vain, nasty, petty, tyrannical, vicious, cowardly, morbidly sensitive, and self-contradictory .... He is a sick and spiteful man. And yet Dostoevsky approves of him .... For ... in the very marrow of that cold and malignant spite is a principle precious for him and for Dostoevsky: freedom.[86]

[82.] Again, p. 234.

[83.] And again, p. 234.

[84.] P. 17.

[85.] P. 284.

[86.] *Dostoevsky: The Major Fiction* (Cambridge, Mass.: MIT Press, 1964), p. 39.

Leatherbarrow touches on a point made by Bercovitch, but divides author and protagonist: "Dostoevsky's dislike of scientific determinism was as keen as the Underground Man's, but that does not imply that he sympathized with the alternatives offered by his hero."[87] Merrill also sees a division: "In a footnote to the first section of *Notes from Underground*, the editor [i.e., Dostoevsky] immediately makes clear that he wants to be carefully separated from the writer of the notes."[88] Cardaci points out obviously enough that Dostoevsky is not his persona.[89] Traschen says: "In the final analysis, though ambivalent towards the underground man, the Raskolnikovs, the Ivan Karamazovs, Dostoyevsky is unequivocal about the fallacy or 'sin' of merely intellectualizing."[90] Dostoevsky is not his protagonist, but nonetheless Jones asserts that "clearly Strakhov, allowing for some subjective exaggeration, was right in pointing to a kinship between Dostoyevsky and his hero."[91] And finally Avrahm Yarmolinsky takes Traschen's comment several steps further as he says that the underground man is an intellectual type Dostoevsky abhorred because he is cut off from the soil.[92] If Dostoevsky abhorred the underground man as a solipsistic intellectual, he nonetheless was himself an intellectual, who apparently felt himself in touch with the soil, and surely in the underground man's striving to free himself from scientific determinism Dostoevsky was in accord. There is a definite kinship, and furthermore the underground man and Dostoevsky are akin in having markedly sado-masochistic characters. For Mark Kanzer points out that "Only by his illness and general masochism, by turning his aggression against himself, was Dostoyevsky able in real life to avoid the fate of his criminal characters."[93]

There is too much I don't like about the underground man for me to exclaim melodramatically that I am the underground man. But nonetheless I am *an* underground man. Aging, solitary, highly educated and trapped in a low-level job, with the best love of my life lost to me almost five years ago, willing to be in contact with people but finding few interested and few worth communicating with, I have been driven into the underground. Contextualism, the world view I accept, stresses in its earlier developments close contact with people in order to create historic events, but in its later

87. Pp. 64-65.
88. P. 510.
89. P. 248.
90. P. 373.
91. P. 55.
92. *Dostoevsky: Works and Days* (New York: Funk & Wagnalls, 1971), p. 195.
93. "Dostoyevsky's Matricidal Impulses," *Psychoanalytic Review*, 35 (1948), 124.

developments (since the work of Stephen C. Pepper) it recognizes the difficulties in establishing close communication and marked alienation from the majority of people. In this desert of Amerika, I think anyone who is fully aware has to go underground. I think that this is true even if one has someone to love or a spouse and family. It may be true in Europe, and it is certainly true in many countries in other parts of the world. At any rate, I am underground, wishing I weren't, longing for companionship, but finding people mostly unwilling and mostly hopelessly inappropriate to be close to.

VI

THE BROTHERS KARAMAZOV: A BIBLIOGRAPHIC
ESSAY AND A CODA

This study is based on a limited amount of material in two respects. First, as I know only elementary Russian and no other Eastern European language, material in those languages was unavailable to me. Secondly, I have researched only what material was available in one university library collection. The material discussed in this essay all turns out to be in English with the exception of one essay in French. While studies in Russian probably notice nuances in Dostoevsky's language that would escape most Western writers, it is my hope that the material I discuss is broadly representative of criticism on *The Brothers Karamazov*.

First, a brief summary is in order on Dostoevsky's sources. These are discussed by Alexandra H. Lyngstad in *Dostoevskij and Schiller*[1] and by B. G. Réizov in "Affrontment de traditions littéraires dans *Les Frères Karamazov*."[2] There are allusions to Schiller's play *Die Rauber* and to his poetry throughout *The Brothers Karamazov*. Ivan is on the surface like the dutiful son Karl Moor in *Die Rauber*, and Mitya is like the undutiful Franz Moor. But of course Ivan wishes his father's death, and Smerdyakov acts on Ivan's wish, so Ivan also resembles Franz. This is noticed by both writers.[3] Anyone who has read Schiller's poetry knows how idealistic it is, and not just the famous "An die Freude." And there is plenty of religious idealism of course in Dostoevsky's novel. Réizov also

---

[1.]   Slavistic Printings and Reprintings, 303 (The Hague: Mouton, 1975).
[2.]   Trans. Ann Pascal, *Revue de littérature comparée*, 46 (1972), 219-41.
[3.]   See Lyngstad, p. 55, and Réizov, p. 225. Mitya is also like Karl Moor in his idealism. And Mitya's idealism is undercut by his own behavior.

discusses Zola's influence on Dostoevsky, and the pages on Schiller in his essay are fine but circumscribed. Lyngstad's two chapters on Schiller and *The Brothers Karamazov* are splendid and full of comparisons. She points out, for instance, that Schiller's play *Don Carlos*, influenced the Grand Inquisitor chapter.[4]

Réizov's discussion of Zola's influence on *The Brothers Karamazov* affirms that Dostoevsky was opposed to Zola in everything and yet was interested in him.[5] Réizov points out that

> La théorie du milieu aboutit naturellement à la célèbre formule "Tout est permis", parce que tout est justifié par le milieu, la passion, le désir de la chair.[6]

Then there is Zola's emphasis on heredity, and

> *Les Frères Karamazov*, pour la première fois dans l'oeuvre de Dostoievski, étudient les problèmes de l'hérédité qui ont eu un très grand retentissement dans la littérature de la fin du siècle. Les tares du vieux Karamazov diversement différenciées sont transmises héréditairement à tous ses fils qui les assument comme une malediction familiale.[7]

How much of a curse old Fyodor's genes pass on to his sons is questionable, but heredity does have a prominent role in the novel. Then too Zola comes to mind because of the "débordement des appetits"[8] in *The Brothers Karamazov*. Of course Dostoevsky ultimately rejects Western and liberal ideas,[9] but, as Réizov points out, the influence of Zola is discernible.

The books on Dostoevsky that I have surveyed present a generally sad picture. It seemed for a time that all who wrote or edited books on him were religious zealots. Then I found, towards the end of my search, a few that weren't religious. Examples from a few authors will illustrate the generally deplorable state of Dostoevsky monograph criticism.

Robert Louis Jackson, in *The Art of Dostoevsky: Deliriums and Nocturnes*,[10] says at the end of his chapter on Ivan's rebellion:

---

4. Pp. 49-50.
5. P. 233.
6. P. 230.
7. P. 235.
8. P. 236.
9. P. 240. This of course is common knowledge.
10. (Princeton, NJ: Princeton Univ. Press, 1981).

in its inner content, this rebellion bears witness to man's continual need to rediscover his humanity in himself, to sacrifice himself for others, in short, to imitate Christ.[11]

William J. Leatherbarrow, in *Fedor Dostoevsky*,[12] says:

The dual perception of each of the brothers Karamazov confirms the dualistic nature of man as revealed in the book of Genesis: he is created from both the Holy Spirit and the dust of the earth.[13]

Malcolm V. Jones, in *Dostoevsky: The Novel of Discord*,[14] says of Ivan:

in his confession to Alyosha Ivan declares that he accepts God; it is simply his world that he does not accept. If this is the "real" Ivan it would seem misplaced to call him either an atheist or an agnostic; he would seem rather to be a believer, in revolt against his Creator.[15]

Ivan may well be a kind of believer, but note Jones's blithe assumption that there is a "Creator." Finally, J. Middleton Murry, in *Fyodor Dostoevsky: A Critical Study*,[16] says:

Alyosha in the midst of the welter of his father's swinishness, Dmitri's fever of moral agony and Ivan's torment of the divided person, is, as it were, born good. He is the miracle.[17]

And here we are back in Sunday school.

Two contributions by believers should be noted with more attention. Roger B. Anderson, in *Dostoevsky: Myths of Duality*,[18] despite his wrongheaded emphasis on mythmaking, does emphasize Zossima's heterodoxy:

---

11. P. 334.
12. Twayne's World Authors Series, 636 (Boston: Twayne, 1981).
13. P. 159.
14. (London: Paul Elek, 1976).
15. P. 178.
16. (New York: Russell and Russell, 1966).
17. Pp. 242-43.
18. Univ. of Florida Humanities Monograph Series, No. 58 (Gainesville: Univ. of Florida Press, 1986).

Turning to Zosima's place within the historical *starets* tradition, divergences from the usual mold of Orthodoxy are all the more evident. The *starets* institution is itself a development of the Hesychast movement of the early Eastern church. As a spiritual practice, Hesychasm primarily emphasized the heart, the efficacy of sentiment, and minimized the intellect.[19]

Sergei Hackel's "The Religious Dimension: Vision or Evasion? Zosima's Discourse in *The Brothers Karamazov*," in the anthology *New Essays on Dostoevsky*,[20] shows by its title and its clear statements about given uncertainties how forthright this believer is. Dostoevsky of course gives vast space for doubt in the novel despite its affirmative, idealistic ending. Hackel says in conclusion:

> The would-be prophet had attained his "hosanna", his faith, "through a great furnace of doubt". Yet the doubt had not been left behind. It informs the arguments of Ivan, it gives Zosima's counterweight, that Western monk, the Grand Inquisitor, his haunting and his lasting power. Dostoevsky thus had good reason to emulate the possessed boy's father in the Gospels and to pray, "Lord, I believe; help thou mine unbelief" (Mark 9: 24).[21]

The other monographs vary in quality and concerns. David I. Goldstein's topical *Dostoevsky and the Jews*[22] deals with Dostoevsky's anti-semitism and gives instances of it in *The Brothers Karamazov* that a reader might overlook. Richard Peace's two chapters on the novel in *Dostoevsky: An Examination of the Major Novels*[23] are journeyman work, being in a few places reductive and on the whole competent but without brilliant insights. N. M. Lary's chapter on the novel in *Dostoevsky and Dickens: A Study of Literary Influence*[24] is informative, dealing among other things with the special problem of Russia and Dostoevsky's authoritarianism. André Gide's pertinent chapter in his *Dostoevsky*[25] is very short and superficial. F. F. Seeley's "Ivan Karamazov,"

---

19. P. 122.
20. Ed. Malcolm V. Jones and Garth M. Terry. (Cambridge: Cambridge Univ. Press, 1983), pp. 139-68.
21. P. 165.
22. Univ. of Texas Press Slavic Series, No. 3 (Austin: Univ. of Texas Press, 1981).
23. (Cambridge: Cambridge Univ. Press, 1971).
24. (London: Routledge and Kegan Paul, 1973).
25. Trans. Louise Varèse (New York: New Directions, 1961).

in the *New Essays on Dostoevsky* collection,[26] is a good study, bringing up in passing Ivan's unconscious. Smerdyakov asserts that Ivan is most like his father of any of the sons. Seeley rightly points out the marked differences between old Fyodor and Ivan. Finally, John Jones's *Dostoevsky*[27] is simply awful. Consider, for example, this passage:

> Not talking, not playing billiards, but turning a shop assistant out of his seat. A package under a pillow or a mattress or neither. An alleged question to a peasant coachman. These are mere spoonfuls from the *Karamazov* ocean, but I hope they give some sense and interest to no-frame *(alias* flaunted frame that turns into ghost-frame) and life-simulation in the novel.[28]

And that garrulous garbage was published by prestigious Clarendon Press! A lot of passages in books and articles have been written on the crucial Grand Inquisitor chapter. The definitive reading of the Grand Inquisitor legend is D. H. Lawrence's "The Grand Inquisitor, by F. M. Dostoievsky" in *Phoenix.*[29] Lawrence's position is summarized in this statement:

> I still see a trifle of cynical-satanical showing-off. But under that I hear the final and unanswerable criticism of Christ. And it is a deadly, devastating summing-up, unanswerable because borne out by the long experience of humanity. It is reality versus illusion, and the illusion was Jesus', while time itself retorts with the reality.[30]

Francis L. Kunkel's "Dostoevsky's 'Inquisitor'; An Emblem of Paradox"[31] leans on Lawrence but comes out emphasizing ambiguity and divided

---

26. See note 20.
27. (Oxford: Clarendon Press, 1983).
28. P. 305.
29. Subtitled *The Posthumous Writings of D. H. Lawrence*, ed. Edward McDonald (New York: Viking, 1936), pp. 283-91.
30. P. 283. Note also this statement (p. 285) on Dostoevsky himself: "As always in Dostoievsky, the amazing perspicacity is mixed with ugly perversity. Nothing is pure. His wild love for Jesus is mixed with perverse and poisonous hate of Jesus: his moral hostility to the devil is mixed with secret worship of the devil. Dostoievsky is always perverse, always impure, always an evil thinker and a marvellous seer."
31. *Renascence*, 16 (1964), 208-13.

loyalties. Philip Rahv's "The Legend of the Grand Inquisitor"[32] is inadequate for two reasons. First, Rahv wants to keep the legend removed (and therefore rendered inefficacious):

> Dostoevsky stands at two removes from the Inquisitor, and Ivan at one remove; and this placing, or aesthetic "distancing," reflects precisely the degree of commitment we are entitled to assume.[33]

Then Rahv wants to make things political. He brings up Dostoevsky's linkage of socialism with the catholic church and, out of the blue, brings up "Russian Christian anarchism."[34] Robert Louis Jackson, again writing in *The Art of Dostoevsky: Deliriums and Nocturnes*,[35] and Jacques Catteau, in "The Paradox of the Legend of the Grand Inquisitor in *The Brothers Karamazov*" in *Dostoevsky: New Perspectives*,[36] are typical of the other writers on the legend. Catteau says:

> With his Grand Inquisitor, Ivan grips the world in the cold rings of despair. With his Christ, before whom the doors of the dungeon open, Ivan creates a breath of hope.[37]

And Jackson unabashedly asserts this: "Dostoevsky . . . maintains that man cannot stand alone; but the deity before whom he bows is Christ—aesthetically, transcendent Beauty, the ineffable Ideal."[38]

Quite a number of articles on *The Brothers Karamazov* are of course written by religious zealots, and as we've been to Sunday school already, I'll pass over those without comment. But though religious views are prominent among the articles, the articles contain the best work on the novel probably because quite a number were written by people who come particularly to this novel without being Dostoevsky specialists with religious investments to make. To complete this survey of criticism on *The Brothers Karamazov*, I'll proceed in three stages: (1) a survey of a number of articles, (2) a closer

---

[32] *Partisan Review*, 21 (1957), 249-71.
[33] P. 253.
[34] P. 264.
[35] See note 10.
[36] Ed. Robert Louis Jackson, Twentieth Century Views (Englewood Cliffs, NJ: Prentice-Hall, 1984), pp. 243-54.
[37] P. 252.
[38] P. 344.

look at two flawed articles of special interest, and (3) broad coverage of six essays which include the best work on the novel.

What follows in this stage of my essay is random topically and in approach, so there is no way for there to be real organization. George Gibian's "The Grotesque in Dostoevsky"[39] sees old Fyodor as a "buffoon."[40] It is nice to find at least one critic who doesn't cast moral judgment on him. But Gibian takes it as fact that old Fyodor violated stinking Lizaveta, the mother of Smerdyakov, and that isn't known for sure. Reed B. Merrill, in "Ivan Karamazov and Harry Haller: The Consolation of Philosophy,"[41] points to Ivan's unwittingly causing the death of his father as evidence that he has opened "the doors to a vision of brute lawlessness and immorality,"[42] which is not only a moralistic judgment but also does not necessarily follow. Merrill also seems to see passion leading to lamentable results. Maximilian Braun, in "*The Brothers Karamazov* As An Expository Novel,"[43] mentions that Dostoevsky, in his preface, asserts that Alyosha is his main hero. Braun asserts that Mitya is the hero of the main plot, and Braun seems to have more justification on his side than Dostoevsky. Nathan Rosen's "Why Dmitrii Karamazov Did Not Kill His Father"[44] makes a number of telling points, but in seeing Katya as the guardian angel who prevents such a crime, Rosen is going too far. Smerdyakov kills old Fyodor before Mitya has a chance to. Rochelle H. Ross, in "Who Is Ivan Karamazov?"[45] emphasizes that in his struggle between doubt and faith Ivan is very like his creator, Dostoevsky. In Roger B. Anderson's "The Meaning of Carnival in *The Brothers Karamazov*"[46] the comparison of old Fyodor and Zossima makes a few points but is on the whole very strained. Kevin Corrigan's "Ivan's Devil in *The Brothers Karamazov* in the Light of a Traditional Platonic View of Evil"[47] says almost nothing that one could not infer from reading the appropriate chapter of the novel. Janine Langan, in her generally unsatisfactory essay "Icon vs. Myth: Dostoevsky, Feminism and Pornography,"[48] does rightly say: "He [Dostoevsky] has a unique, lurid talent for arousing in his reader the

---

[39.] *Modern Fiction Studies*, 4 (1958), 262-70.

[40.] P. 264.

[41.] *Comparative Literature Studies*, 8 (1971), 58-77.

[42.] P. 65.

[43.] *Canadian-American Slavic Studies*, 6 (1972), 199-208.

[44.] *Canadian-American Slavic Studies*, 6 (1972), 209-24.

[45.] *Forum (Houston)*, 8, No. 2 (1970), 39-43.

[46.] *Soviet and East European Journal*, 23 (1979), 458-78.

[47.] *Forum for Modern Language Studies*, 22, No. 1 (1986), 1-9.

[48.] *Religion and Literature*, 18, No. 1 (1986), 63-72.

peculiar thrill linked to successful sado-masochist fantasies . . . ."[49] This is particularly evident when he inserts in the novel the story about a little boy torn to pieces by vicious dogs. Michael Wreen's "Monadology" of *The Brothers Karamazov*,"[50] not successful in terms of its thesis, does make this telling statement:

> Dmitri's relationship with Katerina, a relationship continually and subtly swinging between the poles of hate and love, power and obedience, covetousness and sacrifice, baseness and nobility, is a relationship in which each character is grappling with him- (or her-) self just as much as he (or she) is striving to come to terms with the other.[51]

I could go on, but by this point randomness has probably been carried far enough.

The two essays that I've singled out for special attention are Mark Spilka's "Human Worth in *The Brothers Karamazov*"[52] and Joyce Carol Oates's "The Double Vision of *The Brothers Karamazov*."[53] Spilka makes a number of good points. For instance, he says:

> Plainly Ivan's estimate of adulthood derives, at least in part, from his own neurotic feelings.
>
> More importantly, it derives from the Rousseauistic view of man which Dostoevsky often entertained. The general strength of the nineteenth-century belief in childhood innocence, and its threatened corruption by adult society, needs no documentation . . . . He was appalled, however, by his own discovery of sexual feeling in children . . . . [54]

Ivan of course suffered as a child and is obsessively upset about the suffering of children. Spilka rightly observes that Zossima's sermon "runs toward . . . diffusion and boring prolixity."[55] Farther on, he dwells on Mitya:

[49.] P. 65.
[50.] *Philosophy and Literature*, 10 (1986), 318-24.
[51.] Pp. 321-22.
[52.] *Minnesota Review*, 5 (1965), 38-49.
[53.] *Journal of Aesthetics and Art Criticism*, 27 (1968), 203-13.
[54.] P. 41.
[55.] P. 42.

His [Dostoevsky's] readiness, at this stage of life, to confront neurotic feelings may well explain the Freudian cast of Dmitri's redemption, his decision to forgo parricide and incest, and (in effect) to seek a fitting mate, as in the normal maturation process. At precisely this stage his affection for Grushenka emerges: she is no longer the object of obsessive lust; she becomes, as it were, a different person, and through her Dmitri becomes a man . . . . His Madonna-Sodom split is apparently healed; he is the first of Dostoevsky's characters to overcome the compulsive swings of dualism.[56]

Because he is put on trial for a murder that he didn't commit and sentenced to prison, Mitya is obviously a profoundly changed man. But is he "redeemed"? It is extremely dubious to take how a man behaves in such a terrible situation as indicative of much except the incredible pressures put on him by his situation. Then Spilka finds an analogous hope for the schoolboys at the ending but doesn't buy Alyosha's religiosity. I think that that hope is more than a bit sentimental.

Oates explores the doubling of characters, the fathers and "fathers" for instance, to a considerable extent. But her essay, even more than Spilka's, is one with a thesis:

Whenever the anonymous narrator speaks as a person, the novel sinks to a simplistic moral level which clearly seems the level Dostoevsky wants, since he feels the necessity of bringing his novel back again and again to this level, no matter how far it has soared from it. When the narrator disappears and the characters come alive, in long, rambling, and often hysterical speeches, the novel attains a vitality that wrenches its parts out of relationship to the whole . . . . Two visions—one existential and tragic, the other Christian and comic—are unequally balanced in this novel and do not in my opinion resolve themselves.[57]

This statement should be taken in conjunction with one at the end:

Or does it [the novel] mock its very intentions, containing within it an anti-novel, a tragic vision of life that bitterly opposes the joy of the ending?[58]

---

[56] Pp. 47-48.
[57] P. 203.
[58] P. 213.

I don't find the narrator quite as bad as Oates does. To be sure, the narrator is a Christian and does, for instance, moralistically speak of old Fyodor's "turning his house into a sink of debauchery."[59] But when Ivan has his dream of the devil, the narrator does not freakishly call it God's punishment of Ivan but naturalistically explains it as the result of brain fever. The narrator is, however, but an element in Oates's argument. When she speaks of parts being out of relationship to the whole, she identifies herself as an organicist critic looking for an overarching unity, something not to be expected from that loose, baggy monster, the novel. But now we come to the thrust of her argument, the supposititious two novels in one. In *The Brothers Karamazov* there are of course Christian comic elements, existential questioning, and tragedy for Mitya in his imprisonment and for Ivan in his mental illness. However, instead of finding and opposing two novels in one, Oates should be opposing novel and novelist. She either doesn't know or disregards Lawrence's position that the novel, if genuine, is to be trusted and that the novelist, who brings some moralistic or metaphysical or whatever kind of baggage to his novel, is not to be trusted. Also, this novel, grim as it is, contains besides its religiosity and tragic vision some hearty sensuality. In her last statement Oates is right to ask if Dostoevsky mocks his intentions. He certainly does. But instead of groping about with the idea of an anti-novel within this novel, Oates should have applied to the novel the Panzaic principle,[60] which of course she doesn't know.

I now proceed to the six essays among which the best work on the novel is to be found. Freud's "Dostoevsky and Parricide"[61] only in two places speaks of *The Brothers Karamazov*, but as it is Freud's study of parricide, the single most momentous event of the novel, I include it in the discussion. Freud calls the novel "the most magnificent . . . ever written,"[62] and certainly that is not an extravagent claim. Further on he says:

---

[59] Citations from Dostoevsky in my text are to *The Brothers Karamazov*, trans. Constance Garnett (New York: Random House, 1950). P. 6. Further page references are given in the text.

[60] By the Panzaic principle ideals, of either author or characters, in some great novels and some other literary works are undercut and deflated by the realities elsewhere in the work. See Wayne Burns, *The Panzaic Principle* (Vancouver, BC: Pendejo Press, n.d.), passim. See also the discussion of the Wendy Bowman Morris essay further on.

[61] *Dostoevsky: A Collection of Critical Essays*, ed. René Wellek, Twentieth Century Views (Englewood Cliffs, NJ: Prentice-Hall, 1962), pp. 98-111.

[62] P. 98.

> It can scarcely be owing to chance that three of the
> masterpieces of the literature of all time— . . . *Oedipus Rex* . . . ,
> *Hamlet* and . . . *The Brothers Karamazov*—should all deal with the
> same subject: parricide. In all three, moreover, the motive for the
> deed, sexual rivalry for a woman, is laid bare.[63]

But even more important is what he says about Dostoevsky, whose father
was murdered:

> His early symptoms of deathlike attacks [of epilepsy] can . . . be
> understood as a father-identification on the part of his ego, which
> is permitted by his super-ego as a punishment. "You wanted to kill
> your father in order to be your father yourself. Now you are your
> father, but a dead father"—the regular mechanism of hysterical
> symptoms. And further: "Now your father is killing *you*."[64]

Freud even asserts that Dostoevsky, who was almost executed and served
years in prison, had to get himself punished for his death wish against his
father. It should be noted that Smerdyakov, the murderer in the novel, is,
like Dostoevsky, epileptic. The last part of Freud's essay is an analysis of
Stefan Zweig's story, "Vierundzwanzig Stunden aus dem Leben einer Frau."
This doesn't seem to fit very well, but the ostensible link is gambling in
the story and Dostoevsky's gambling mania. However, according to Harry
Slochower's "Incest in *The Brothers Karamazov*,"[65] it deals with the novel in
a veiled way. Slochower says:

> That the master of the oedipal analysis should have missed the
> major incest figure in the novel seemed incredible to me. Careful
> analysis discloses, however, that Freud after all does "analyze"
> Katya. But he does so "unconsciously" . . . .[66]

Katya is an incest figure because she resembles Mitya's mother. Slochower's
argument runs thus: Katya also resembles the woman in the Zweig story;
Freud's wife, Martha, also had some resemblance to Katya; therefore, in
analyzing the story, Freud was doing unconsciously what he couldn't bear
to do consciously.

---

[63] P. 107.

[64] P. 105.

[65] *American Imago*, 16 (1959), 127-45.

[66] P. 139.

In what ways does Katya resemble Mitya's mother? Slochower says: "The identification of Katya with Mitya's mother lies above all in their attempt to dominate their men."[67] Moreover, Katya becomes a kind of goddess figure. Also, she is aristocratic and "noble" seeming. At times she tries to be a "sister" to Mitya but reverts to her tyrannical "love." Slochower shows another incestuous link:

> Mitya is obsessed with the feeling that *he can [be] rid of his "debt" to Katya only by giving her the money which he has inherited from his mother and which his father, is withholding from him.*[68]

Grushenka is of course the other incest figure. Slochower incisively observes: "It is of some significance that Mitya's attitude towards Grushenka is a transference of Katya's to him."[69] He means by this that both will tolerate rival lovers. The only other lover that Mitya can't tolerate is his father, and with him the conflict is open and clear-cut. Using a number of elements from the plot to marshal his arguments, Slochower produces an essay that is revelatory and first rate.

Neal Bruss, in his essay "The Sons Karamazov: Dostoevsky's Characters as Freudian Transformations,"[70] defines the transformation technique in this way:

> Freud represented a repressed thought as an underlying clause or sentence, introduced the ordinary negative as "the hall-mark of repression," and then derived explicit symptoms from the clause by negating one or another of its parts.[71]

Bruss summarizes the ways in which the sons (he includes Smerdyakov) respond to old Fyodor thus:

> Two sons display exaggerated activity: Dmitri quarrels hysterically with his father, and Alyosha attempts to express "active love" as his Elder charges him. The other two sons tend toward passivity: Ivan condescends to the other characters, and Smerdyakov plays the part of a cowardly, simple-minded,

---

67. P. 131.
68. P. 134.
69. P. 135.
70. *Massachusetts Review*, 27 (1986), 40-67.
71. P. 41.

eunuch-like epileptic. Both types of roles require character-distortion. The two passive sons diminish themselves, Ivan by a cynic's refusal to act. Smerdyakov by the appearance of innocence. The two active sons distort the character of their father by magnification, Dmitri in his extreme vulnerability to his father's provocation, and Alyosha in raising for himself a second, saintly father, the Elder, in the image of his mother.[72]

In his further discussion Bruss makes refinements about each man that are more markedly transformational, more in line with Freud's study of Dostoevsky from which Bruss draws the transformation process. This also is a first-rate essay, but somehow it isn't as exciting as Slochower's.

Gilbert D. Chaitin's "Religion as Defense: The Structure of *The Brothers Karamazov*"[73] also uses Freud and is concerned with ways to deal with the Oedipus complex. In the course of the essay a number of assorted and quite valid points are made. But his thesis is contained in this statement:

> In the world of the novel itself, Dmitri's defense is one of the least satisfying, for unless the desire for self-sacrifice is coupled with the renunciation of woman, as in Zossima's and Alyosha's cases, in the long run the defense must fail.[74]

In his youth Zossima did have murderous impulses in a rivalry over a woman, and Chaitin's thesis works quite well in his case. But Alyosha thinks seriously of marrying Lise. And his parricidal impulse seems feeble at best. Chaitin's thesis works more dubiously in connection with him. In his concluding statement Chaitin generalizes:

> if we step outside the world of the novel, we must acknowledge that this sense of super-individual guilt [Zossima's] is merely an evasion of the truth, a neurotic way of not coming to grips with one's own unconscious parricidal wishes, whose result can only be increased misery for the individual and eventually for society at large.[75]

I have seen Chaitin write more satisfying essays than this one. Yet he makes some points in it.

---

72. P. 48.
73. *Literature and Psychology*, 22, No. 2 (1972), 69-87.
74. P. 86.
75. Again, p. 86.

Geoffrey Carter's "Freud and *The Brothers Karamazov*"[76] is one of the best things done on the novel. Carter is a bit too fearful of the unconscious—though from this novel we do see what murderous impulses can arise from it. Otherwise, he does unexceptionable work. Note, for instance, what he says about Katya:

> Katerina would like to think of her self-sacrifice for her father as the noblest thing she has ever done; but the fragility of that concept is clearly shown by her falling into fits of hysterics when Grushenka, her feared rival for Dmitry, throws it into her face that she, Katerina, was once willing to sell herself to a man. The strength of the hysteria shows that Grushenka has touched on Katerina's repressed motivation for coming to Dmitry.[77]

And, to conclude, there is this statement about Ivan:

> Ivan's behavior in court, so terrible and so true, so clearly seen by Dostoevsky, does not, of course, prove the existence of God or a higher order of being that triumphs over the atheistic free-ranging intellect, nor yet that man has an innate morality that he will attempt to defy at his cost; rather, it shows that no amount of applied introspection can release us from our conditioning by our infantile past, that the morality introjected at that state, to form the super-ego, is intransigent and harsh in its demands, and asks that we do not even think of crimes against the members of the nuclear family, that to think such things is as terrible as to do them. Ivan's morality, like everyone's, is entangled with erotic elements that he is not aware of, but which Dostoevsky goes out of the way to make the reader aware of.[78]

Wendy Bowman Morris's "Panzaism and Dostoevsky"[79] is a first-rate contribution to studies of the novel. Consisting of minimal text interspersed with well-chosen quotations, the essay begins by opposing the senses ("the 'guts are always right'")[80] to the intellect. And the sensuality of old Fyodor, Mitya, and Grushenka does undercut all the intellectual poses in the novel.

---

76. *Literature and Psychology*, 31, No. 3 (1981), 15-32.

77. P. 18.

78. P. 27.

79. *Paunch*, No. 22 (1965), 47-56.

80. P. 47.

Paul Green

Morris goes on to point out, employing a quotation from Ortega y Gasset, that even the most realistic novels allow us to escape from our painful, and most probably painfully banal, reality. But a novel such as *The Brothers Karamazov*, even as it is a kind of escape, plunges us much of its way into a very disturbing "reality." Morris gets to the crux of the matter when she says: "In the approach of idealistic intellectuals who want to change the world by reason, he [Dostoevsky] saw only futility . . . ."[81] The reality, or "reality" if you will, of the novel undercuts not only the rational idealism of Ivan but also the religious idealism of Zossima and Alyosha. Specifically, the legend of the Grand Inquisitor undercuts Alyosha and Dostoevsky's religious ending. And the mental illness of Ivan undercuts his attempt to live so exclusively from the mind.

Quite a number of the critics, including the religious ones, make perfectly valid points about *The Brothers Karamazov*, but, in surveying the criticism that I could, I have found only a dozen or so pieces that have overall merit. This is a sad commentary on the critics. In the process of studying the criticism and rereading the novel, I have come up with some observations on the characters that are more or less independent of the criticism. These observations constitute the coda and ending of this essay.

Old Fyodor does some reprehensible things. He takes the money of his first wife, Mitya's mother. He treats his second wife, a submissive creature, so badly that at times she is in states of insanity. He neglects his sons and lets them be brought up by other people. He does give some money to Mitya, but he gives nothing to Ivan or Alyosha. The critics seem to hate him as much as Mitya and Ivan do. But old Fyodor, buffoon and drunken slob that he is, lives for women, and that is to his credit. He hoards his money so that he'll be able to spend it on women in his advanced years. Whatever he may have done, he has the right priorities.

Zossima, Alyosha's surrogate father, is likeable considering that he is a religious figure. This can be seen by contrasting him to the puritanical Ferapont. He is heterodox and pantheistic. He says: "Fathers and teachers, I ponder 'What is hell?' I maintain that it is the suffering of being unable to love . . . ." (p. 387). And that I can agree with wholeheartedly. But still he is religious, and there are three things he says and does that I don't like. First, he says: "he [the monk] is responsible to all men for all and everything . . . ." (p. 194). In a world such as this it is well to be responsible only to the people close to one. Secondly, when he was much younger, he urged a friend who had murdered to confess. And finally, he talks about "sins." Sympathetic as he is, Zossima still has most of the limitations of religion.

[81.] P. 49.

124

The childlike Mitya by his deeds does his best to get himself sent to prison. This is because he is almost pure id with scarcely any ego defenses. In saying this I don't mean to be cautionary. It is simply an observation about him and the consequences of his actions. From the erratic nature of his behavior some readers of the novel might conclude that he isn't very bright. But that isn't so; he is a good judge of character. After Grushenka has loved him for an hour and then tortured him, Mitya realizes that she too is having an inward struggle. And he infers that his father's facial expression would be different if Grushenka were with him. Then too he rightly infers that old Samsonov is really laughing at him. Anal in his violence and violent tendencies, Mitya is scarcely anal at all about money. I have as hard a time as the prosecuting attorney does believing that Mitya actually saved fifteen hundred roubles of the money he got from Katya. But of course he is spending that riotously when he is arrested.

The brilliant Ivan tends to think others' intelligence is substandard. To him Smerdyakov, whom he can't stand, is mentally deficient until Smerdyakov becomes pressing and Ivan reluctantly concedes that Smerdyakov is cleverer than he had thought. And he tries to belittle his devil, a most articulate, cosmopolitan, and companionable fellow. Ivan loves Katya from an early point in the novel and, despite several statements to the effect that he doesn't care for her, he loves her steadily. He loves her so intensely that at times he feels a murderous hatred of her. She of course is the wrong choice for anyone despite her beauty, being sadomasochistic and hysterical. But then Ivan lives so much in his mind that he isn't the most suitable choice for a mate. At the end Katya has him, as she has taken the mentally ill man into her home.

Alyosha, Dostoevsky's supposititious hero, is the least vivid and living of the brothers.[82] But there are relatively gentle and loving believers such as he. He claims to be an authentic Karamazov sensualist, but aside from his interest in Lise and his being stirred when Grushenka sits on his knees, there seems little evidence of it. Or, rather, he seems to be basically homoerotic.[83] He undoubtedly loves Zossima more than anyone else, and he seems to have too strong an interest in young boys.

Grushenka loves Mitya wholeheartedly and devotedly from the time of his arrest, but before that she is almost cruelly fickle and capricious. However, it may be true that she was loving her Polish "officer" all along

---

82. Marc Slonim, in the introduction to this edition of the novel, says (p. xiii): "Alyosha's image is somewhat pale and lacks the forcefulness of Dostoevsky's transgressors and rebels."

83. Alyosha's homoeroticism was made conscious for me by José Vargas.

and just playing with others. She is indeed sensual, but there is a calculating, anal side to her too. Mitya says of her: "I knew, too, that she was fond of money, that she hoarded it, and lent it at a wicked rate of interest, that she's a merciless cheat and swindler . . . ." (p. 140). This goes far beyond just being prudent about money, but it should be noted that she was abandoned in her teens and left destitute and after that experience began saving money.

Crime and Punishment is a brilliant study of Raskolnikov, but it remains mostly the study of one character. *The Brothers Karamazov*, Dostoevsky's final work, contains a number of brilliant character studies and is altogether a larger and more ambitious book, the finest he wrote.

VII

AESTHETICIZED VIOLENCE:

"IN DER STRAFKOLONIE"

Whereas the country doctor in Kafka's "Ein Landarzt" badly needs to *make* some connections, we now encounter a man, the officer of "In der Strafkolonie," who wants very badly to *have* connections. In his need to have connections he is like K. in *Das Schloss*, but while K. is engaged in a sort of *Schattenkrieg*, there is on the contrary no lack of real contention in "In der Strafkolonie." Also, the contention in this story is conclusive to the extent that the officer commits suicide and in so doing acknowledges the end of the old regime—even if the ending is rendered somewhat ambiguous by the explorer's flight. "In der Strafkolonie" is exemplary in that it not only depicts contention and violence but also in that the contention is *about* violence itself and the situation obliges serious reflection. In this story violence doesn't just happen spontaneously. The suddenness of the officer's decision to commit suicide is nullified by the implacably bizarre logic which leads him to that decision.

One of the most pressing concerns of modern artists and intellectuals, in the main, is the havoc created and the toll taken by the rapid implementation and increasing development of technology in advanced societies. The defeat of the machine in the story, the recent habit of speaking of our time as a postindustrial era, the demonstrable superiority of many technological means to get things done, and the uneasy feeling that humanists get somewhat hysterical on the question of technology cannot negate the fact that there are clear dangers in the technologized state. Concern on the matter is vital because the technologists, by and large, are given over to functional preoccupations. To the functionalist effective performance is the highest good. All other concerns are secondary.

According to Herbert Marcuse, the result of technological functionality is insidiously effective domination:

> Qualitative change . . . involves a change in the *technical* basis on which this society rests—one which sustains the economic and political institutions through which the "second nature" of man as an aggressive object of administration is stabilized. The techniques of industrialization are political techniques as such, they prejudge the possibilities of Reason and Freedom.
>
> . . . as all freedom depends on the conquest of alien necessity, the realization of freedom depends on the *techniques* of this conquest. The highest productivity of labor can be used for the perpetuation of labor, and the most efficient industrialization can serve the restriction and manipulation of needs.
>
> When this point is reached, domination—in the guise of affluence and liberty—extends to all spheres of private and public existence, integrates all authentic opposition, absorbs all alternatives. Technological rationality reveals its political character as it becomes the great vehicle of better domination, creating a truly totalitarian universe in which society and nature, mind and body are kept in a state of permanent mobilization for the defense of this universe.[1]

Though Marcuse speaks of an era of more effective controls subsequent to Kafka's time, the officer Kafka creates in "In der Strafkolonie" has a mentality so warped that it shows functionalism at its utmost—albeit not at its most subtle. His vicious friendliness and his attachment to the torture machine would be almost pathetic were it not that he is ultimately a dehumanized monstrosity. The old commandant whose memory the officer so venerates must have been the kind of power-wielder Marcuse has in mind. The officer we meet in the story is no more than a well-"sold" follower.

From the officer's pride in the machine, it might be taken for his own invention. But that honor belongs to the deceased commandant, who was "'Soldat, Richter, Konstrukteur, Chemiker, Zeichner'"[2] all in one. And as

---

1. *One-Dimensional Man: Studies in the Ideology of Advanced Industrial Society* (Boston: Beacon, 1964) 18.

2. Citations from "In der Strafkolonie" in my text are to Kafka's *Sämtliche Erzählungen*, ed. Paul Raabe (Frankfurt am Main: Fischer, 1970). Here p. 103. Further page references will be given in the text.

the officer explains the workings of the machine to the visiting explorer, the system's pervertedly reversed priorities appear in the fact that the harrow has long needles, which do the writing on the body, and short ones, which squirt out water to wash away the blood and keep the machine clean. The implicit principle—whereby the machine is of inestimable value and human life and suffering inconsequential—is confirmed by an incident which happens after the condemned man is actually put in the machine. Nauseated by the felt gag placed in his mouth, he starts to vomit, and the officer quickly pushes his head to the side to keep his beloved machine clean. Then the soldier almost reflexively comes over to clean up the mess with the man's shirt.[3]

But the "writing" process is no useless show of the ingenious, as the officer takes pains to point out. The writing—indeed the overall functioning of the machine—does not do with slow elaborateness what a bullet could do with efficiency. The process provides "enlightenment." The long ordeal is a means of *teaching* the dying man:

> "Begreifen Sie den Vorgang? Die Egge fängt zu schreiben an; ist sie mit der ersten Anlage der Schrift auf dem Rücken des Mannes fertig, rollt die Watteschicht und wälzt den Körper langsam auf die Seite, um der Egge neuen Raum zu bieten. Inzwischen legen sich die wundbeschriebenen Stellen auf die Watte, welche infolge der besonderen Präparierung sofort die Blutung stillt und zu neuer Vertiefung der Schrift vorbereitet. Hier die Zacken am Rande der Egge reissen dann beim weiteren Umwälzen des Körpers die Watte von den Wunden, schleudern sie in die Grube, und die Egge hat wieder Arbeit. So schreibt sie immer tiefer die zwölf Stunden lang. Die ersten sechs Stunden lebt der Verurteilte fast wie früher, er leidet nur Schmerzen. Nach zwei Stunden wird der Filz entfernt, denn der Mann hat keine Kraft zum Schreien mehr . . . . Wie still wird dann aber der Mann um die sechste Stunde! Verstand geht dem Blödesten auf. Um die Augen beginnt es. Von hier aus verbreitet es sich. Ein Anblick, der einen verführen könnte, sich mit unter die Egge zu legen. Es geschieht ja weiter nichts, der Mann fängt bloss an, die Schrift zu entziffern, er spitzt den Mund, als horche er. Sie

---

3.   This incident is singled out with slightly different emphasis by Mark Sacharoff in "Pathological, Comic, and Tragic Elements in Kafka's 'In the Penal Colony,'" *Genre* 4 (1971): 400. He comes closer to what I am emphasizing here in his introduction, pp. 392-93.

haben gesehen, es ist nicht leicht, die Schrift mit den Augen zu
entziffern; unser Mann entziffert sie aber mit seinen Wunden.
Es ist allerdings viel Arbeit; er braucht sechs Stunden zu ihrer
Vollendung. Dann aber spiesst ihn die Egge vollständig auf und
wirft ihn in die Grube, wo er auf das Blutwasser und die Watte
niederklatscht. Dann ist das Gericht zu Ende, und wir, ich und
der Soldat, scharren ihn ein." (p. 108)

Lida Kirchberger says, it seems to me rightly:

> The machine in the penal colony, as has been observed by
> others, is clearly marked as the central figure of the story, while
> supporting roles only are assigned to human characters, even to
> the officer who, by his knowledge of and involvement with the
> machine, comes foremost.[4]

Despite the officer's averring that the "enlightment" almost tempts the
observer to get under the harrow, what he describes is a singularly hideous
means by which to teach a "lesson."[5] And because the conception that
suffering is a good teacher is so pervasive, outright condemnation of the
torture process is less "moralizing" than necessary self-defense. Observe,
for example, what Leah Hadomi says:

[4.] *Franz Kafka's Use of Law in Fiction: A New Interpretation of* "In der Strafkolonie,"
Der Prozess, *and* Das Schloss, New York University Offendorfer Series, n.F.,
Bd. 22 (New York: Peter Lang, 1986) 19.

[5.] A number of critics touch on the religious implications of this story, but the most
systematic treatment, to my knowledge, is Edwin R. Steinberg's "The Judgment
in Kafka's 'In the Penal Colony,'" *Journal of Modern Literature* 5 (1976): 492-514.
He deals with the script-scripture question in several places (see esp. pp. 493-94,
496-98, and 499-500) in a flatly one-to-one allegorical fashion, whereas he
should have kept his interpretation at a suggestive or allusive level–and pointed
out how devastatingly vicious religious legalism becomes by suggestion in the
story. On the other hand, Clayton Koelb, in "'In der Strafkolonie': Kafka and
the Scene of Reading," *German Quarterly* 55 (1982):515, does point out the
viciousness: "The prisoner rebels, but the role is now to be forced upon him
by the execution machine, which not only rides him but even penetrates his
flesh, makes him even less than animal, makes him an object upon which to
inscribe commandments, a matrix upon which is to be impressed the stamp
of rigid authority." Elizabeth Dalton, in "Kafka as Saint," *Partisan Review* 54
(1987): 411, says: "Perhaps the most horrifying aspect of the story is not the

All three spheres, the Utopian, Dystopian and Anti-Utopian are embodied in the story ["In der Strafkolonie"] and express the complexity of the Utopian dilemma. The Utopian sphere is centred around the Old Commandant who had invented the machine to implement the Utopian ideal. At the centre of the Dystopian sphere stands the machine, to which the island society has become subservient since the death of the Old Commandant. It is a world of mechanical function deprived of its spiritual content. The centre of the third sphere—the Anti-Utopian—is the hedonistic tea-house in which the grave of the Old Commandant serves as a table.[6]

Some liberal religious people are very nice. A conservative religious person such as Hadomi can only be called perverted. The teahouse is the only pleasant and human place on the island.

The officer needs the explorer, who is to be his connection. Despite the fact that the old commandant and the officer are chillingly representative

---

penal colony, nor the officer, nor even the structure of the torture machine. Rather it is the details of the machine's mode of operation and the quality of the attention devoted to them. That attention is avid, finicky, sensual." Peter U. Beicken, in *Franz Kafka: eine kritische Einführung in die Forschung* (Frankfurt am Main: Athenäum, 1974) 290, says: "Der 'Widersinn als Aufbau-Prinzip' enthüllt die 'radikale Pervertierung der Idee der Gerechtigkeit,' und der Sinn der Selbst-Hinrichtung des Offiziers liegt darin, dass sich eine so pervertierte Rechtsanfassung selbst aufheben muss." Beicken is quoting one W. Biemel.

6. "The Utopian Dimension of Kafka's 'In the Penal Colony,'" *Orbis Litterarum* 35 (1980): 236. (See again the comment on Steinberg in note 5.) Two other critics also take abominable positions. A. P. Foulkes, in *The Reluctant Pessimist: A Study of Franz Kafka*, Stanford Studies in in Germanics and Slavics (The Hague: Mouton, 1967) 114, says: "The reality of existence, hideous though it may be, is man's only path to *Erkenntnis*, and hence to a knowledge of the spiritual world. *Erkenntnis*, it will be remembered, is not merely the desire for death, but the awareness that eternity can be reached through destruction of self." This is what Freud would call the death wish or death instinct with a vengeance. Meno Spann, who is *sometimes* good, says in *Franz Kafka*, Twayne World Authors Series, 381 (Boston: Twayne, 1976) 110: "Kafka makes it an important point of the story that neither the officer conducting the execution nor his revered old commandant should be considered lawless tyrants or sadists. Like the inventor of the execution machine, the officer is merely practising 'sacred cruelty,' his one concern in life being justice." That people can take such positions seems almost incredible.

of the modern functionalist mentality, Kafka presents their system as one jeopardized rather than in firm control. The new commandant opposes the torture-machine process, and popular support for the process has also dwindled.[7] Thus the officer hopes to persuade the presumably prestigious explorer to intercede on his behalf. This the explorer refuses to do, and directly the officer releases the condemned man and becomes himself the victim of the machine, which all but destroys itself in the process of executing him. The victory is almost ridiculously easy and decisive, but the question remains as to how representative the development in the story is. "In der Strafkolonie" was written at the time when World War One was starting, and clearly historical developments have shown—fluctuations in intensity and variations in visibility being granted—a marked increase in barbarism since that point in time. And some determined sociological

---

7. Kafka, by the defeat of the officer and the torture machine, makes his story more hopeful and positive than contemporary (to his writing of the story) conditions were as Ulrich Schmidt observes in "Tat-Beobachtung: Kafkas Erzählung 'In der Strafkolonie' im literarisch-historischen Kontext," in *Franz Kafka und die Prager Deutsche Literatur*, ed. Hartmut Binder (Bonn: Kulturstiftung der Deutschen Vertriebenen, 1988) 58: "Das 'Unschuldige' und doch 'Peinliche' von Kafkas Erzählung liegt darin begründet–und das ist meine These–, dass dieser wenige Wochen nach Ausbruch des Ersten Weltkriegs verfasste Text im skrupellosen Fanatismus des Offiziers und im Skeptizismus des abwägenden Reisenden die unmenschlichen Konsequenzen enthüllt, welche der vitalische Lebenskult nach der Jahrhundertwende dann zeitigte, als seine literarisch chiffrierten Ideale 1914 im Sinne der militärischen Radikalisierung der allgemeinen Lebensverhältnisse ausgelegt wurden." Kafka was deeply influenced by Dostoevsky especially at the time of the writing of this story and *Der Prozess*. W. J. Dodd, in "Dostoyevskian Elements in Kafka's 'Penal Colony'" *German Life and Letters* 37 (1983): 11, says: "It has been observed that in writing 'In der Strafkolonie' Kafka drew on his knowledge of Dostoyevsky's Siberian exile, but very little attention has been given to Dostoyevsky's possible influence on the story beyond this seemingly incidental level." He says further (also p. 11) and to the point here: "Of all the particulars of Dostoyevsky's penal servitude, the constellation of the lenient Commandant and the vindictive second-in-command Krwtsov was perhaps the most suggestive for Kafka." He also draws a parallel between Dostoyevsky's Grand Inquisitor and Kafka's old commandant (p. 17). Martin Beckmann, in "Franz Kafkas Erzählung 'In der Strafkolonie': ein Deutungsversuch," *Wirkendes Wort* 39 (1989): 389, says: "Die Vorliebe des neuen Kommandanten für Hafenbauarbeiten zeigt die Alternative zum Apparat des Verfahrens und zum Weg des Offiziers."

research has shown how thoroughly functionalist-operationalist controls have permeated "peacetime" or "productive" activity to the end that men serve machines rather than the reverse.[8] But that is almost a donnée when disastrously exploitative politico-economic systems are in force. Despite its dénouement, "In der Strafkolonie" is prophetic, and a statement made relative to the story over four decades ago is just as true now as it was then: "our everyday world has taken on all the characteristics of the penal colony, and if we accept its values, we are the executioners and the executed."[9]

While the torture machine represents technological encroachment at a highly menacing level, the officer who is so proud of the machine represents the kind of person who is dangerous precisely because his level of awareness prevents him from being anything but blindly functionalist.[10] The officer's words and actions also show how much danger there is in allowing a person of limited awareness and warped personality to have even a restricted amount of power. Becoming a military officer, for example, is no extraordinary feat, and if his assignment is of the "right" sort, an ordinary

---

8. Marcuse's *One-Dimensional Man* is one such analysis, and sufficiently sociological. Less developed but as bitterly indicting is a short passage (pp. 94-95) in The Frankfurt Institute of Social Research's *Aspects of Sociology*, trans. John Viertel (Boston: Beacon, 1972). Though its approach is more descriptive than judgmental, Erving Goffman's *The Presentation of Self in Everyday Life* (Garden City, NY: Anchor-Doubleday, 1959) is relevant here as it touches often on the need to "act" in relating, on the rule of the performance principle, and on contrived and unwitting inauthenticity. See, for example, pp. 64 and 70.

9. Wayne Burns, "'In the Penal Colony': Variations on a Theme by Octave Mirbeau," *Accent* 17 (1957): 51. Walter H. Sokel, in *Franz Kafka: Tragik und Ironie: zur Struktur seiner Kunst* (München: Albert Langen und Georg Müller, 1964) 115, also observes how timely and prophetic the story is but with this distinction: "Selbstverständlich ist die STRAFKOLONIE kein Vorläufer der Konzentrationslager. Denn während die Konzentrationslager auf Unterdrückung und Vernichtung des Individuums ausgingen, ist es der Strafkolonie um die Verklärung des Individuums zu tun." But his distinction is weakened immensely by the fact that sure death follows the "enlightenment."

10. Sacharoff (p. 398) specifically speaks of his "lack of awareness" and says shortly before that the officer is "consistently insensitive to the human implications of the victim's impending torture and death." When Dale Kramer asserts in "The Aesthetics of Theme: Kafka's 'In the Penal Colony,'" *Studies in Short Fiction* 5 (1968): 366, that the officer is "a hero," about the kindest thing one can conclude is that Kramer is to be pitied.

military officer may be able to possess decisive powers. Such is the case with Kafka's officer. In terms of his duties as a military man, he functions very capably. Yet despite his ability to perform "normally," he is an utter madman. It is the very fact that he can function—albeit in a horrendous sort of job—and that he doesn't take himself to be the king of England, for example, which prevents his madness from being obvious.

Of course, his choice of death for his kind of principles points to derangement. However, my point is that regardless of his suicide he is deranged. His death, like the statements he makes, gives evidence of his rigid determination to *interpret* his job and do it as he feels compelled to rather than to change with the times, the commandant, or the situation. I say this not to try to establish willingness to please as an absolute principle but rather to indicate the extent of the officer's rigidity, conservatism, and blindness. It is out of the question for him to go along with the new commandant and to take an interest in the harbor works. He has a cause—the measure of his madness is the undeniable justness of that cause in his eyes—and he feels obliged to fight for that cause, and with self-pitying pride, against the odds. His assurance that the explorer will see things his way and that the explorer's support will overwhelm the new commandant is likewise a measure of his madness. When the explorer refuses, the officer is seemingly struck with a kind of reality he cannot face and so chooses death rather than giving up his more hideous kind of reality, writing "justice" into the bodies of living men. And the "justice" done is in keeping with the officer's mad certainty of his rightness. Judge as well as executioner, he does not allow for ensnarling defenses and appeals. "'Die Schuld ist immer zweifellos'" (p. 104). The case of the condemned man in question shows that even neglect of duty is sufficient cause for the officer to carry out judicial torture.[11]

Though the officer is singlemindedly obsessed with his torture process, he yet has enough presence of mind to take close heed of "the other side." Even while he confidently prepares the explorer to come to his and the system's defense, the officer gives out signals to show that he is cognizant of possible counterarguments. Clearly he must be echoing some of the

---

[11.] James B. Street's "Kafka Through Freud: Totems and Taboos in 'In der Strafkolonie,'" *Modern Austrian Literature* 6.3-4 (1973): 93-106, deserves notice insofar as it connects this story to the mythical "primal crime" and the questions of guilt, revolt, etc. Jürg Beat Honegger, in *Das Phänomen der Angst bei Franz Kafka*, Philologische Studien und Quellen, 81 (Berlin: Erich Schmidt, 1975), gives one of the unequivocal condemnations of the machine and the old order. Pp. 241-42 are particularly relevant here.

objections of the new commandant. Similarly, his taking heed of objections indicates that he is worried. Also, he manifestly wants to show the explorer how aware he is of what people in general think. Thus he peppers his appeal to the explorer with possible counterarguments and misgivings:

> "Seine [the new commandant's] Berechnung ist sorgfältig; Sie sind den zweiten Tag auf der Insel, Sie kannten den alten Kommandanten und seinen Gedankenkreis nicht, Sie sind in europäischen Anschauungen befangen, vielleicht sind Sie ein grundsätzlicher Gegner der Todesstrafe im allgemeinen und einer derartigen maschinellen Hinrichtungsart im besonderen . . . . Sie haben allerdings viele Eigentümlichkeiten vieler Völker gesehen und achten gelernt, Sie werden daher wahrscheinlich nicht mit ganzer Kraft, wie Sie es vielleicht in Ihrer Heimat tun würden, gegen das Verfahren aussprechen. Aber dessen bedarf der Kommandant gar nicht, Ein flüchtiges, ein bloss unvorsichtiges Wort genügt . . . . Sie werden etwa sagen: 'Bei uns wird der Angeklagte vor dem Urteil verhört', oder 'Bei uns gab es Folterungen nur im Mittelalter'." (pp. 112-13)

The officer states that the new commandant doesn't yet dare to halt the torture process but plans to use the explorer's negative opinion to the end of stopping the process. But his cleverly planned surprise for the commandant elicits a refusal from the explorer which takes the officer by surprise.

The officer's decision to become himself the victim of the machine is ostensibly a choice of death rather than "dishonor." More importantly, his choice to suffer and die in the torture machine after making codified and ritualized sadism a way of life tends to confirm the psychoanalytic pronouncement that a person who is markedly sadistic or masochistic will inevitably be driven to the other extreme too—that, in effect, there is a sadomasochistic character type.[12] Less clinically, the case of the officer suggests that one whose manner of life is effectively life-denying can be so far gone in hatred of life that he welcomes the opportunity to die. In this light the defeat of the officer and the torture system provides an excuse to escape from a life the officer perhaps finds undesirable at best. To some these statements might seem highly conjectural, but it is at least clear that the officer's actions turn in the end reflexively back on him.

---

12. See Wilhelm Reich, *Character Analysis*, 3d enl. ed., trans. Theodore P. Wolfe (New York: Noonday, 1949) 210-11.

In its more customary manifestations at least, sexuality does not play a prominent part in this story. Yet the intimations of sexuality which are there can be significant. For one thing, women are a nuisance to the officer. There are, of course, women of one kind and another. The officer's account of the popularity of the executions during the lifetime of the old commandant indicate that men, women, and children flocked to witness them. The old commandant, like the new one, had his entourage of ladies. In his pointed contrast of past and present ways, the officer provides evidence of what is certain—that women, as well as men, can be life-deniers and willing supporters of whatever regime is in power. But what the story points to subtly, in seemingly casual details and in the complaints of the officer, is women's more or less intuitive recognition that a choice of death-dealing and death-in-life is a rejection of them. That the officer "hatte zwei zarte Damentaschentücher hinter den Uniformkragen gezwängt" (p. 118) seems to indicate that some women have tried to distract and beguile him. And this is presumably the case—even though these handkerchieves turn out to be gifts for the condemned man. Also, at the time the condemned man, strapped in the machine, vomits, the officer annoyedly complains:

> "Habe ich nicht stundenlang dem Kommandanten begreiflich zu machen gesucht, dass einen Tag vor der Execution kein Essen mehr verabfolgt werden soll. Aber die neue milde Richtung ist anderer Meinung. Die Damen des Kommandanten stopfen dem Mann, ehe er abgeführt wird, den Hals mit Zuckersachen voll." (p. 110)

Furthermore, the officer feels that the women deserve much of the blame for jeopardizing his precious torture system: "'Soll wegen dieses Kommandanten und seiner Frauen, die ihn beeinflussen, ein solches Lebenswerk . . . zugrunde gehen?'" (p. 111). In particular, he fears some women will prevent the explorer from speaking on his behalf. Though overemphasis on the women's softening influence verges on the sentimental, such touches as these that Kafka inserts from time to time indicate that the women of the penal colony recognize the officer's loving attachment to the machine and the torture process is not only a rejection of them but also almost an attempt to nullify womankind. And neither the widely known study of Heinz Politzer nor that of Wilhelm Emrich appears willing to acknowledge as much.[13]

---

[13]. Indeed, there is generally little criticism which takes account of the intimations of eroticism in this story. Politzer, in his *Franz Kafka: Parable and Paradox*, rev. ed. (Ithaca, NY: Cornell UP, 1966) 109-10, takes note of the feminine presence

Even someone so free of illusions as Lawrence's Loerke[14] might possibly be jolted if he saw, by means of the officer and his machine, where his mechanizing aesthetic leads at its utmost. But then again probably Loerke would know it only too well. And the officer clearly has an "aesthetic" attitude of a dismal sort in that his emotions are entirely engaged with the machine and the process. If he loves at all, he apparently loves the old commandant's memory and himself insofar as there is narcissism-identification with the deceased leader, his code, and his invention. More rudimentarily, he has gone asexual—with implications borne along, by his example, to the effect that asexuality can be maintained only at a high psychic cost.

The incident that gets the condemned man into the straits he is in is one in which he is the victim of violence, and it has ramifying significance in that it shows that the officer is not the only sadist in the penal colony:

"Er [the condemned man] hat nämlich die Pflicht, bei jedem Stundenschlag aufzustehen und vor der Tür des Hauptmanns zu salutieren . . . . Der Hauptmann wollte in der gestrigen Nacht nachsehen, ob der Diener seine Pflicht erfülle. er öffnete Schlag zwei Uhr die Tür und fand ihn zusammengekrümmt schlafen. Er holte die Reitpeitsche und schlug ihm über das Gesicht. Statt nun aufzustehen und um Verzeihung zu bitten, fasste der Mann seinen Herrn bei den Beinen, schüttelte ihn und rief: 'Wirf die Peitsche weg, oder ich fresse dich.'—Das ist der Sachverhalt." (p. 105)

When being slashed across the face with a whip is appropriate punishment for the failure to perform a duty of "blatant uselessness,"[15] the new commandant has far more reforming to accomplish in the colony than merely abolishing the use of the machine. But mere reforms can never eradicate the fundamentally inhuman practices built into any military system. They can only make things less bad.

---

in the story but *seems* to end up saying that it is decadent and debilitating. Emrich, in his *Franz Kafka: A Critical Study of His Writings*, trans. Sheema Zeben Buehne (New York: Ungar, 1968) 274-75, notices the erotic but sweeps it away in a reductive rejection of the new order (as well as the old) because it has "sacrificed redemption" (p. 275). My rejection of his rejection of the new order should not be taken as unqualified support for it–as my remarks further on make clear. Sokel (pp. 112-13) has the significance of the ladies more in focus.

14. In *Women in Love.*
15. Politzer, p. 101. He also points out that the man can scarcely be said to be menacing his superior despite the threat.

It is perhaps not entirely clear precisely what attitude Kafka took towards what he depicts in this story,[16] but it does need to be pointed out—especially as I have taken a hard line against the officer—that Kafka makes efforts to complicate the reader's response. He does so through his characterizations of the condemned man and the explorer. The condemned man is initially made to seem utterly harmless, and as things develop, it becomes clear he is rather obtuse. Even as he is singularly unterrified by his clearly impending fate, he is intently curious about the machine and the process. (Through the condemned man—and to a degree the officer's unwitting self-revelation—the Kafkaesque comic filters into this grim story.)[17] By these means, by his playful wrestling with the soldier after his release from the machine, and by his desire to linger at the scene of the suicide, we come to see this man as a sadly brutalized specimen of humanity.

The explorer comes to witness the execution only because he has been requested to and not out of a compelling interest. Initially impatient with the officer's explanations, he gradually becomes intrigued and finally involved as he determines that he won't speak in favor of the torture process. In refusing to help the officer, the explorer holds fast to his liberal humanitarian views and clings to his safeguarding status as observer and outsider. But the swift decision of the officer to sacrifice himself in the machine and the machine's malfunctionally swift killing of the officer draw the explorer into the middle of a chain of events he had no thought of being part of.[18] These developments bring about his hurried departure in the boat for the steamer and his attempt to sever all connections with the island and the machine by preventing the soldier and the condemned man

---

[16] Opposite views as to what Kafka must have been thinking are expressed by Ronald Gray and Helmut Richter. In *Franz Kafka* (Cambridge: Cambridge UP, 1973) 99, Gray says that "in allowing the explorer to make off for his ship, Kafka lent all the weight of the story to the officer. In the balance of the whole, the impression is created, that the alternative to the officer's conviction is merely the pusillanimity of the explorer, and this gives a certain grim majesty to the officer's dead face." In *Franz Kafka: Werk und Entwurf*, Neue Beiträge zur Literaturwissenschaft, 14 (Berlin: Rütten und Loening, 1962) 127, Richter cites the explorer's feeling of having experienced too much and having no fear about wavering in his answer to the officer's plea in support of the thesis that "Kafkas neue Position ist die des Reisenden."

[17] See Sacharoff passim on the comic and see p. 403 on the condemned man (and the soldier).

[18] However, the explorer's refusal to help the officer saves the life of the condemned man.

from coming too.[19] Though Kafka was dissatisfied with that ending,[20] as such it indicates that spatial separation from the island will not obliterate from the explorer's active mind memories of what happened there. And the explorer is little beyond a registering mind—and like the officer at least insofar as he is not in touch with the springs of life. As Wayne Burns says:

> Kafka's explorer is throughout most of the story an impartial scientific observer, a personification of John Dewey's liberal intelligence. He is therefore not a three-dimensional character, but a kind of disembodied mind, and his function is to observe and comment upon what he finds in "the penal colony."[21]

The explorer wants to be a person whose judgments don't count. He is therefore perhaps like many people. To say that we are all guilty is patently wrong, but it is clear that our actions, and at times our failures to act, have *consequences*, often consequences we cannot foresee. Evidently the explorer, in turning himself into a registering mind, has had the illusion that he can avoid being a consequential person—and surely his flight is a frantic attempt to perpetuate that illusion. But Roy Pascal says rather unconvincingly: "his [the explorer's] panic flight from the colony makes

---

19. In "Kafka's 'In the Penal Colony,'" *Explicator* 24 (1965): item 11, Kurt Fickert rejects allegorical interpretations of the story and emphasizes the explorer's using flight as a solution to avoid "the paradoxes of truth." Leonard R. Mendelsohn's "Kafka's 'In the Penal Colony' and the Paradox of Enforced Freedom," *Studies in Short Fiction* 8 (1971): 309-16, develops the thesis about the explorer's unwilling involvement to which I am indebted. (But on the basis of the explorer's being called generally *der Reisende* Mendelsohn concludes wrongly that he is merely a traveler. On p. 100 of the cited edition he is called the "Forschungsreisende[n]," and cumulative detail on him in the story leaves little room for doubt about his being an explorer.) Also, James Rolleston, in *Kafka's Narrative Theater* (University Park: Pennsylvania State UP, 1974) 97, says this: "The machine has destroyed, in addition to itself, the identity of both officer and explorer; as it reveals the completeness of the latter's involvement in his identity as an observer, the destruction of the machine precludes a resumption of any 'real' detachment."
20. See Gray, pp. 99-100.
21. "Kafka and Alex Comfort: The Penal Colony Revisited," *Arizona Quarterly* 8 (1952): 105. Burns's omission of an expanded commentary on the explorer as unwilling participant appears to be related to his anxiousness to get on to his primary concern, Comfort's *On This Side Nothing.*

us dubious about the superiority of his humanitarian principles to the inhuman but selfless devotion of the officer."[22]

As the story develops, liberal reformism wins out over conservatism in extremis, yet the liberal new commandant's unwillingness to act against the torture process until the time is "right" points to his complicity in the officer's way of operating. This does not mean that the liberal (or, more so, the radical) should try to save the world but rather, minimally, that he should try to save himself. For acquiescence commits him to maiming and mutilation—both psychic and physical—in the larger penal colony which is modern industrial or post-industrial society. Obliquely, the story indicates that liberals, in their attentiveness to finding the "right" time to stop the torture-executions, fail to see that slashes with whips are more than "discipline." And that is a measure of their limitations. And in the oblique commentary on disembodiment, gradualism, and disembodied gradualism is one main thrust of "In der Strafkolonie."[23]

---

[22] *Kafka's Narrators: A Study of His Stories and Sketches* (Cambridge: Cambridge UP, 1982) 61.

[23] When Kurt Tucholsky, in "'In the Penal Colony,'" *Critical Essays on Franz Kafka,* ed. Ruth V. Gross (Boston: G. K. Hall, 1990) 157, says: "The traveller and the condemned man and the soldier on duty watch powerlessly [as the officer dies]. And then they still go around in the city and then the traveller gets on a boat and leaves. And suddenly the book is at an end. You need not ask what it is all for. It is not for anything[,]" he shows an appalling lack of understanding of this story. On another note, Roy Pascal, in "Kafka's 'In der Strafkolonie': Narrative Structure and Interpretation," *Oxford German Studies* 11 (1980): 123, rightly says: "Two impulses bring me to consider Kafka's 'In der Strafkolonie.' The first is dismay at the persistent tendency to interpret this tale as an allegory of faith, guilt, crucifixion, against which I already protested in 1956 in my book *The German Novel* and according to which, with varying degrees of subtlety, the Officer is elevated to the rank of sacrificial hero or even Christ and the Old Commander is looked on as a symbol of Jehovah, while the arbitrary sentence and penal torture are held to reflect man's original sin and redemption." Pascal's article should have been read by Ernst Loeb, who in "Kafkas 'In der Strafkolonie' im Spiegel 'klassischer' und 'romantischer' Religion," *Seminar* 21 (1985): 139-40, maintains that the old commandant and the officer are akin to "classical" religion and the new commandant akin to "romantic" religion. But at least it must be said that the old commandant was very like the vicious Jehovah.